CRACKING
THE CODE

Also by Thom Hartmann

CRACKING THE CODE

HOW TO WIN HEARTS, CHANGE MINDS, AND RESTORE AMERICA'S ORIGINAL VISION

THOM HARTMANN

Berrett–Koehler Publishers, Inc.
San Francisco
a BK Currents book

Berrett-Koehler Publishers, Inc.
235 Montgomery Street, Suite 650, San Francisco, CA 94104-2916
Tel: (415) 288-0260   Fax: (415) 362-2512   www.bkconnection.com

Ordering Information

Quantity sales. Special discounts are available on quantity purchases by corporations, associations, and others. For details, contact the "Special Sales Department" at the Berrett-Koehler address above.

Individual sales. Berrett-Koehler publications are available through most bookstores. They can also be ordered directly from Berrett-Koehler:
Tel: (800) 929-2929; Fax: (802) 864-7626; www.bkconnection.com.

Orders for college textbook/course adoption use. Please contact Berrett-Koehler: Tel: (800) 929-2929; Fax: (802) 864-7626.

Orders by U.S. trade bookstores and wholesalers. Please contact Ingram Publisher Services, Tel: (800) 509-4887; Fax: (800) 838-1149; E-mail: customer.service@ingram publisherservices.com; or visit www.ingrampublisherservices.com/Ordering for details about electronic ordering.

Berrett-Koehler and the BK logo are registered trademarks of Berrett-Koehler Publishers, Inc.

Printed in the United States of America

Berrett-Koehler books are printed on long-lasting acid-free paper. When it is available, we choose paper that has been manufactured by environmentally responsible processes. These may include using trees grown in sustainable forests, incorporating recycled paper, minimizing chlorine in bleaching, or recycling the energy produced at the paper mill.

Library of Congress Cataloging-in-Publication Data
Hartmann, Thom, 1951–
    Cracking the code : how to win hearts, change minds, and restore America's original vision / by Thom Hartmann.
    p. cm.
    Includes bibliographical references and index.
    ISBN 978-1-57675-458-0 (hardcover : alk. paper)
    ISBN 978-1-57675-627-0 (pbk. : alk. paper)
    1. United States—Politics and government—2001– 2. United States—Politics and government—20th century. 3. Liberalism—United States. 4. Communication in politics—United States. 5. Communication—Psychological aspects. 6. United States—Politics and government—Philosophy. 7. Hartmann, Thom, 1951–
    8. Radio personalities—United States—Biography. 9. Psychotherapists—United States—Biography. I. Title.
    E902.H373 2008
    320.97301'4—dc22
                                                                    2007025814

13 12   11   10   09   08   10   9   8   7   6   5   4   3   2   1

Interior design and composition by Gary Palmatier, Ideas to Images.
Elizabeth von Radics, copyeditor; Mike Mollett, proofreader; Medea Minnich, indexer.

This book is dedicated to Stan and Cindy Hartmann
and to my mother, Helen Jean Hartmann.

A NOTE TO THE READER

This book is written in a new language. Every word means precisely what it says. The tools of communication revealed herein are also used in its writing. You may spot many of these on your first read through, although they will probably be most visible, most clearly heard, and most easily picked out on a subsequent reading.

CONTENTS

FOREWORD

JIM HIGHTOWER

If Jefferson, Madison, Adams, and the boys—the founding fathers—could see what today's leaders have done with their historic handiwork, they'd be scratching their white powered wigs in befuddlement.

How, they'd ask, did America go from "life, liberty, and the pursuit of happiness" to torture, repression of dissent, and pursuit of empire? How did "promote the general welfare" get twisted into tax giveaways for the superrich while millions of children are left with no health coverage? How did "We the people" become they the corporations?

Past leaders who tapped into America's enormous potential for economic fairness, social justice, and opportunity for all have been supplanted by a new breed of cynical manipulators who trade in fear: color-coded fear of foreign madmen; fear of losing your job, home, and health insurance; fear of fear; fear of a Black preacher, for Godssake!

What happened? The fearmongers—striving to impose both a right-wing and a corporate agenda—learned the importance in our culture of telling a story. Underlying their story is a scary worldview teaching that people—that is, "others," "strangers," "them"—are evil at heart and should be treated with suspicion. Forget " Love thy neighbor." Keep your eyes on that SOB! Also central to their story is the pernicious notion that, far from all of us being in this together, each of us is on our own, and everybody must grab as much as they can, as fast as they can.

So these plutocrats, autocrats, theocrats, and kleptocrats spun Horatio Alger tales that glorified barons of commerce and the rise of dot-com billionaires; their newspapers and television stations extolled the privatization of all things public; laissez-faire ideologues were lionized, while unionists and environmentalists were trivialized; they wallowed piously in stories of "family values," even as they proselytized against getting involved in "socialistic" concerns for the larger human family; and they painted images of foreign enemies wielding weapons of mass destruction, as well as bamboozling us with fantasies for neer-do-wells here at home who are out to take our property and livelihoods.

The Powers That Be and their Republican enablers are still churning out meticulously-constructed, focus-group-tested messages that perpetuate fear and aim to make us think that what they want is what we want.

So, where are the Democrats? Where is the liberating, uniting, energizing, progressive story of America, the storyline on which our great country was founded, the ongoing democratic message that leads us toward a just and hope-filled future?

Too often, our story is buried in talking points, a deluge of facts, and a plethora of platform planks. A great grassroots visionary and friend of mine, Van Jones, heads the Ella Baker Center for Human Rights in Oakland, California. Encouraging liberals to reach out to people with more than statistics and power-point presentations, Van notes that Martin Luther King Jr. did not say: "I have a … position paper."

No, Rev. King had *a dream*, and he painted it beautifully, memorably for us in words.

Enter Thom Hartmann—a radio talkshow host, journalist, psychotherapist, and communications expert who has thought a lot and learned a lot about talking to regular folks—that is, the hoi polloi, the rank and file … you and me.

On his daily Air America radio broadcast, Thom makes a point of inviting "The Enemy" onto his show, both as guests and as callers. He has learned their spin, cracked their code, and he has brought us this book to explain how we can do the same.

Keep in mind, this book is not about pointing fingers. After all, as Thom says, "we're all just human here," and everyone votes with the intention of building a society in which their children can grow up safe, healthy, and happy. The problem is that the people at the top—the puppeteers of Corporate America and the Republican party—manipulate the truth to advance their repressive, avaricious, anti-democratic agendas.

Through radio transcripts and historical examples that span back to the 1600s, Thom exposes the inner mechanisms of conservative storytelling and explains exactly how Republicans try to use fear to trump home. Thom dissects a handful of recent campaigns, including the Republican Party's casting of John Kerry a "flip-flopper" in the 2004 presidential election, and—more devastatingly—Bush's manipulation of 9/11 to justify an invasion of Iraq (which, Thom points out, is no longer a war but an occupation).

If We the People are to reclaim the power that corporations and right-wing governments have long usurped, it's time to take action. Our politicians can't save us, no matter how persuasive an orator or how experienced a decision-maker sits in the Oval Office. The burden lies on every individual to absorb the lessons of Thom's book and spread the liberal story far and wide.

Cracking the Code is more than a book about politics, more than a book about communication. It's a book about all the ways you and I can connect with each other to build a better society based on the values of our nation's founders. We have the ability and responsibility to take Thom's belief to heart—that how we communicate dictates how we live, which in turn shapes our world—and *act*. Reading this book is the first crucial step in that direction.

INTRODUCTION

TALKING THE TALK

Communication leads to community, that is, to understanding, intimacy, and mutual valuing.

— ROLLO MAY

My wife, Louise, and I live atop 30 feet of water, 100 feet from shore, in a houseboat on a river in Portland, Oregon. One day I stepped out our back door onto the floating deck that serves as our backyard and found myself confronting a very upset Canada goose. He bobbed his head up and down, lifted his wings to make his body look larger and more intimidating, and ran straight at me, hissing and trying to nip at me.

Observing this behavior my comedian friend Swami Beyond-ananda (Steve Bhaerman), who was visiting us that week, named the bird Goosalini.

I had no idea why this psycho goose was attacking, but there was no mistaking what Goosalini was trying to communicate: *Stay inside that house and don't come out!* I got the message, but I didn't stay inside. Instead, every time I went out to water the plants on my deck, I brought a broom with me to fight off Goosalini.

I found out what was going on a week later, when I learned from my neighbor that a female goose had settled on her back deck, just a few feet from our own, and was sitting on a nest. I realized that Goosalini must have been the proud papa, protecting his territory, and I stopped swatting at him with my broom.

Goosalini has a lot to tell us about communicative strategies. Even though he was just doing what a gander does when he wants a predator to leave—draw attention to himself and away from his

1

mate, attack first and ask questions later—he was able to communicate the "go away" part of his message to me pretty well. We all communicate all the time, even when we don't give much thought to what we are saying or how we are saying it.

Because Goosalini was unable to use what we would call rational powers of persuasion, he communicated by going straight for the more primitive parts of my brain—the parts we shared as human and goose, the center of our gut feelings. The first time Goosalini attacked, I backed off because he was successful in communicating an intent to harm me, which caused me to feel fear, that most primal and visceral of human emotions.

The first key to unlocking the communication code is to understand that when we communicate, *feeling comes first*. Emotions will always trump intellect, at least in the short term.

This emotive form of communication, however, ultimately didn't get Goosalini the response he wanted. On its own the attack wasn't very persuasive. Instead of shooing me away, Goosalini got me angry.

Effective communicators know how to get the response they want because they understand how to tailor a message to the person who's listening. They know the second key to unlocking the communication code: *the meaning of a communication is the response you get.*

Because Goosalini couldn't tell me his story, I had to imagine his story for myself. The first story I came up with was that he was simply a psycho goose, trying to hurt me for no reason I could understand. The second story that I came up with—after talking to my neighbor—was a story of a dad protecting his soon-to-be-hatched goslings. Both stories accurately described what was happening, but the stories led to very different endings. The psycho goose made me angry; the dad goose made me feel protective of Goosalini himself.

In this book I call such stories "maps," and the world the stories describe as "the territory." The third key to unlocking the communication code is: *the map is not the territory.* Each story captures a different piece of reality; no one story captures all of it. *The key to effective communication is to find the best story to use to convey your understanding of the world to the greatest number of people.*

In politics we tell each other stories all the time. If you think about it, politics is really nothing more than a set of stories.

The United States of America began as a story that the Founders and the Framers told about a society that could live in harmony around the principles of life, liberty, and the pursuit of happiness. This country was held together after the Great Depression and through a war by a story told by Franklin D. Roosevelt, which he called the New Deal.

Ronald Reagan told a very different story—one we are still in—that he called the "free market" story. In Reagan's story our corporate CEOs should run our society instead of our elected representatives because, as Reagan pointed out (and believed), "The best minds are not in government. If any were, business would hire them away."

Most of the stories we hear in the media today are scary. We are told to be afraid because the world is a bad place and people are untrustworthy. Every goose is a Goosalini—without understanding why.

These scary stories are profitable to our infotainment industry and to the politicians who are typically allied with the barons of the infotainment industry.

There is a different story, however, in which every Goosalini is a proud papa. It is a story of a world that is interconnected and of people who are fundamentally good. This is the traditional American liberal story, which has been told and understood since the first telling of it during the Enlightenment by thinkers like Jean Jacques Rousseau, John Locke, and Thomas Jefferson. It's the story that reaches directly back to the founding of this country.

My aim with this book is to give you the tools to tell the liberal story—and tell it well. I will show you how the process of communication is coded—actually hardwired into our brains—and help you crack that code to become a brilliant communicator.

First, though, there are a few concepts it's important to master.

Everybody wants the best outcomes, and their behavior reflects the best tools they have to achieve those outcomes.

Another way of saying this is that people always make what they think are the best choices given the circumstances and the tools they have. *All behavior has, at its root, the goal of a positive outcome.*

As a practical statement, this means that conservatives and liberals are both working toward the best world possible.

In 2007 I broadcast my radio program live from the Conservative Political Action Conference in Washington, D.C. Three hours a day for four days, I had one conservative after another on my show, debating the issues of the day with me. As I was the only liberal in a hotel filled with more than 4,000 conservatives, most felt pretty comfortable, and we were often able to meet on a human-to-human level.

One particularly poignant moment came after I'd debated health care with a prominent conservative ideologue, who honestly and strongly believed that if there were absolutely no government interference in the "private marketplace of health care" whatsoever—no Food and Drug Administration (FDA); no pure-drug laws; no regulation of hospitals, doctors, or HMOs; no Medicare or Medicaid—all the "imbalances" in the system would be removed and everybody would end up with access to health care. Our debate was spirited, fast paced, and at times loud. Listeners may have even thought he was occasionally angry with me.

When we were finished and the radio network had gone to the news at the top of the hour and the microphones were turned off, he leaned across the table and said to me, in a soft and friendly voice, as if he didn't want his fellows around to hear: "You know, Thom, you and I want the same things. We both want our children to live in a world at peace. We both want everybody to be healthy and to be cared for when they're sick. We both want to eliminate hunger and poverty in the world. We both want a clean environment, security in old age, and protections from the unexpected dangers of life."

He took a breath, straightened up a bit, and added: "We just differ on how best to achieve those goals. I think the free market will make it all happen if we restrict government to its core function of armies and police. You think these social goals can be achieved with the help of government. But we're both good people who love our families and just want the best. We differ on the means, not the ends."

He was so right.

Of course, there is the occasional sociopath among us (Dick Cheney comes to mind), but I'd argue that they're the exception that proves the rule. At our core we're all essentially interested in the same outcomes.

And we can begin to persuade others of our point of view only when we respect and understand theirs. This establishes the rapport that makes communication possible.

WELL-FORMED OUTCOMES ARE DESIRABLE.

If we're going to set out to change another person's behavior by changing their mind about something, we want the outcome of that new behavior to be useful to both them, us, and everything and everybody else involved. In its largest sense, this is a form of *ecology check*. In the most direct sense, what this means is that we're trying to achieve what's referred to in psychology as a "well-formed outcome." It works. It's sustainable. It accomplishes a new goal.

WE ADD TOOLS BUT NEVER TAKE AWAY TOOLS.

One of the essentials to ensuring a well-formed outcome is to be continually expanding—rather than contracting—the sphere and the collection of behaviors of each person with whom we come into contact.

Understanding that *all* behavior—no matter how dysfunctional or destructive it may seem—has at its core the desire for a positive outcome, you'll quickly understand why, when we try to take behaviors *away* from people, we meet resistance. Instead of trying to stop or delete or prohibit behaviors, it always works better to offer people new and additional, more useful behaviors.

At the smallest level, this means instead of telling children to "stop" doing something in the living room, it's more effective to help them "start" doing something else in the backyard. People will always be receptive to new options, new tools, and new behaviors. It's always more effective to say, "Start this," than to say, "Stop that."

On a larger scale, this illustrates why our government's "War on Drugs" is so dysfunctional. Most illegal (and much legal) drug use is a response to despair, apathy, or boredom. And most illegal drug selling is a response to a lack of other economic activities. Most drug dealers are simply entrepreneurs who lack other, more appropriate means to make money. When we understand this, we realize that providing small-scale entrepreneurial opportunities within a legal context would be far more effective than prison at stopping the illegal drug trade. We saw this writ large during Prohibition (1920–1933) and its immediate aftermath, although most people alive don't remember that time.

On the largest scale, this is often the story of immigrants. When Irish Catholic immigrants came to America in droves in the early 1800s, escaping the potato famine and British oppression, they were viewed by the WASPs already living here as a new "criminal class." Entire books were written about the inherent criminality of the Irish genetics and culture. But the simple fact was that their large numbers drove up the supply of labor, which drove down the price of labor, producing more people than jobs and more poorly paying jobs than well-paying ones. The result was widespread poverty, which lead to widespread crime.

By the 1880s the Irish Catholics, particularly in areas like Boston and Philadelphia, were into their second and third generations. They were Americans. Their numbers were stabilizing, their wages were rising, and suddenly they weren't the criminal class anymore. That role went to the new immigrants of the 1880s from Italy—which produced another generation of speculative writings about the Sicilian gene and the native criminality of Italians and their "mafia culture."

In each case, when people are given more opportunities—more tools—they take them and grow to the next level. When they find tools taken away from them (economic and cultural oppression), they sink into despair and crime.

THERE'S NO FAILURE, ONLY FEEDBACK; NO MISTAKES, ONLY OUTCOMES.

Our biological and psychological/emotional similarities (we're all just human here) mean we're all working toward the same general goals, just using different tool sets and techniques. When things don't work out—personally, politically, or in any other fashion—people who believe they have no other tools, techniques, or options available to them will interpret that outcome as "failure." In fact, there are no failures; there's only feedback. There are no mistakes; there are only outcomes.

Every "failure" can be the germ of a great success. Henry Ford went bankrupt seven times before becoming successful. Thomas Edison tried thousands of filaments before he made a light bulb work. Charles Colson went to prison, and the experience transformed his life in a way that he today believes was both necessary and positive. When we re-understand the results of our actions as "feedback" and "outcomes," new spectrums of options for learning open up to us.

A teacher of mine once told the story of two men who were walking down a rural dirt road. There was a small crack in the road, where a recent rain had cut a 2-inch-wide gulley from one side of the road to the other, and both men, being deep in conversation, tripped on it and fell on their faces.

The man on the right reached over to the side of the road to grab a stick and began beating his own head and shoulders with it. "What an idiot I've been!" he shouted at himself as he repeatedly struck his own head. Meanwhile, the man on the left stood up, saw the crack in the road, made a mental note to look for others in the future, dusted himself off, and recommenced his journey.

The man on the right experienced a mistake in not noticing the crack in the road and a subsequent failure to maintain his balance. The man on the left experienced the outcome of tripping and falling and took the feedback of that experience as an opportunity to learn how to better walk down unpredictable rural dirt roads.

This ties into the concept of more tools and options rather than fewer, and it clarifies the need for well-formed outcomes. The man on the left gained a tool and had the desirable outcome of continuing to walk but with a new and more useful level of knowledge about walking. The man on the right had the poorly formed outcome of self-flagellation and a slowing in his reaching his goal where the road eventually led.

Using These Tools

Communication is value-neutral. It is neither good nor evil. It can be used for either, but, like a screwdriver or a scalpel, is only a tool.

Nonetheless, some people are fearful of open discussions of communication and its code.

Some want to believe that humans are not in any way Pavlovian stimulus/response machines, and thus the idea of enhancing the effectiveness of communication for the purpose of persuasion is all nonsense. They'll often say this, ironically enough, in book reviews published in newspapers or on Web sites funded—including the reviewer's paycheck—by a multi-hundred-billion-dollar industry devoted to (and effective at) producing a specific response ("buy!") to a specific stimulus. The simple reality is that if we didn't react to these tools, the advertising and marketing industry—and, for that matter, the psychotherapy industry—would cease to exist within a year for lack of satisfied customers.

Others fear that teaching people how to be better communicators—particularly in the context of political persuasion—is teaching people how to "manipulate" others. They are right in the technical sense and wrong in the value sense.

For lack of a better word (and we do lack the vocabulary, outside of the very specific vernacular of psychotherapy), we all "manipulate" all the time. It's how we accomplish everything. If you're hungry, you can manipulate an entire multi-billion-dollar industry by offering a few dollars to a clerk in a fast-food restaurant. The result of that manipulation is that you get fed. You manipulated your partner into being your partner, your friends into being your friends, and your pet onto your lap. The only people who don't manipulate are those who are dead.

Manipulate has a negative connotation because one of our most pervasive cultural myths—a victim myth combined with a not-my-responsibility myth—is the belief that we are all totally free agents who act with totally free will yet at the same time our words and actions are only rarely responsible for specific reactions in others. It's such a nice, convenient, comfortable myth set. But the reality is that every stimulus of the world around us—no matter how small or seemingly insignificant—produces a response.

Those who understand this are competent at producing predictable responses. Those who don't are often lost in life and don't know why.

Moving manipulation out of the "practical frame" and into the "value frame," it is true that the tools of competent communication can be used to persuade people in ways that are not in their interest or in the interest of society or the world. Some will suggest that, because of this danger, this book should not exist.

But I can tell you from personal experience that there is little in this book that the senior marketing officials and the most powerful lobbyists for the world's largest corporations don't already know. Frank Luntz and Newt Gingrich (among others) set out, in the 1980s and 1990s, to share much of this information with conservative politicians, and they have used it masterfully since that time (as you'll see in this book).

Psychologically and politically, these are core concepts, whether we're talking about children, adults, politicians, entire groups of people, or even geese.

So it is with respect and hope for a better world that I now hand *you* these tools, trusting that in your hands they will be used for good. The Earth and all life on it need you to be a more competent communicator now at this critical time in our nation's history.

PART I

TELLING YOUR STORY

CHAPTER 1

CRACKING THE
WORLDVIEW CODE

*As Mankind becomes more liberal, they will be more apt
to allow that all those who conduct themselves as worthy
members of the community are equally entitled to the
protections of civil government. I hope ever to see America
among the foremost nations of justice and liberality.*

— GEORGE WASHINGTON

Someone coming to America during one of our national elections
might think politics was a kind of sporting event. They'd see a red
team facing off against a blue team and hear that a team would win
or lose based on how many votes it got.

That kind of thinking got a friend of mine into trouble. Once
an outspoken and proud "dittohead," a few years ago he decided he
was going to instead become a liberal (his wife actually decided it
for him, but that's another story). But this guy tripped up because
he thought that politics was a sporting event with teams that are
just as interchangeable as if a baseball team were to move from
Kansas City to Oakland. He thought it was a matchup with a playlist of issues like Social Security, national health care, and the "War
on Terror." On one side of each issue were conservatives and their
talking points, and on the other side were liberals and their talking
points. He figured all he had to do to switch sides was memorize
a new set of talking points, the way a sports team would simply
change its venue.

But then over lunch, one of us would bring up an issue that wasn't one of the issues for which he'd memorized a new set of talking points. Sometimes it was an issue that didn't even seem obviously political, like why so many coal miners are getting killed in mining accidents[1] or why we're paying to teach kids how to take tests but not paying for music classes.[2] The guy who thought he had gone from being a conservative to a liberal didn't know what to say. Those issues just weren't in his playbook.

A true liberal or conservative, with a grounding in the philosophy and the history of the liberal or conservative worldview, would instantly know how to respond to such issues.

A liberal would put the miners' story inside a bigger story about how corporations are now required by law to care more about profits than people and how the evisceration of the labor movement by Reagan's "War on Labor" and later conservative pro-business efforts have stripped workers of the democratic and balancing power in the workplace (known as *unions!*) to emphasize things like safety.

A liberal might answer the music issue by talking about a child who learned how to read and write after he started playing a musical instrument—how that shows there are different intelligences we all have and can express—and conclude by stressing how important it is that we create an opportunity for every child to realize his or her potential.

There is a story behind every political issue, a story that is either liberal or conservative. Politics is no more and no less than the sum of those stories.

THE COMMUNICATION CODE

To be an effective communicator, we learn *how* to tell a story, *to whom* to tell that story, and *why*.

Everyone is a communicator, and we all communicate constantly. Some of us, like Bill Clinton, Ralph Nader, and Ronald Reagan, are born storytellers and natural communicators. The skill of communication and persuasion seems innate and effortless. Folks like that are *unconsciously competent* at communicating.

Most of us, however, are not very competent at communicating; what's more, we don't *know* we're not competent. We are *unconsciously incompetent.* The challenge we face when we want to communicate effectively is to go from being unconsciously incompetent to being *unconsciously competent.* This involves four stages.

Learning to communicate well is like learning to ride a bike. At first you don't know what it's like to ride a bike (*unconsciously incompetent*); then, when you start learning, you fall off a lot (*consciously incompetent*).

After a while you get the hang of bike riding, but you have to concentrate on pedaling, turning, shifting, and so forth (*consciously competent*).

Then, one day, you are riding around with a friend and you suddenly realize you haven't even thought about being on a bike for the past ten minutes. You know how to ride the bike so well that you can now focus on other things you want to do while you are riding it (*unconsciously competent*). This is true of everything we learn, from walking to talking to typing to reading. And you'll learn the communication code in just the same way:

- Unconsciously incompetent—never thought about the impact of words; wonder why communication often is misunderstood

- Consciously incompetent—become aware of these tools and how often you're not using them or are doing things wrong

■ Consciously competent—start using the tools but have to pay attention; thinking things through before doing or saying them

■ Unconsciously competent—powerful, influential communication becomes second nature

Anyone, with any message, can become an effective communicator. Stephen Hawking, mute and in a wheelchair, continues to influence the entire world with his communications. The communication code itself is politically neutral. It's just a tool.

Combining a competent use of that tool with a good ethical base and a positive vision produces a powerful and useful force. When people combine competent communication with a desire to dominate others or to rule through fear, it often becomes a corrosive force that strikes at the very heart of our democratic republic.

The tools of communication are widely known. I learned many of them from working with Richard Bandler and reading the works of John Grinder, two men who together developed a theory of communication they called Neuro-Linguistic Programming (NLP).[3] Professional message makers like Frank Luntz and Newt Gingrich have studied these tools as well. These message makers have used their knowledge of the communication code to convince average working Americans that middle-class interests correspond with those of global corporations and the mega-wealthy. Luntz, Gingrich, Karl Rove, and others like them—the manipulators of Madison Avenue, Wall Street, and the Bush White House—figured out how to crack the communication code to become masters of political persuasion.

Some politicians' efforts at persuasion are conscious, intentional, systematic, and, of necessity, deceptive because they don't share the worldview held by the majority of Americans. To respond, the rest of us must learn to communicate more effectively.

THE CONSERVATIVE STORY

Much thought and many words have been devoted to the differences between conservatives and liberals, ranging from their temperament to their parenting to their vision of government.

One popular line of thought is that conservatives want a government that's a stand-in for a "strict father" whereas liberals are more interested in a government that plays the role of a "nurturing family." While this may help explain the strain of authoritarian conservatives so well documented by John Dean in his book *Conservatives without Conscience*, it fails to note that the history of the left is littered with equally authoritarian figures, from Leon Trotsky to Joseph Stalin to Fidel Castro. It's an excellent exposition on the authoritarian-seeking personality, but it doesn't address the true historical and modern differences between conservative and liberal thought.

Another popular canard is that conservatives value personal liberty at the expense of the good of society, whereas liberals value social goals above personal freedom. While both sides use this to beat up the other, it fails to explain why such an overgeneralization would even come into being or why most liberals hold personal liberty (a value conservatives claim) as a high value, and most conservatives believe that their worldview will best solve the problems of society as a whole (a value liberals claim).

To truly understand the difference between modern conservative and liberal thought—and policy—it's necessary to step back in time to the beginning of the modern versions of both. They emerged within a generation of each other, in England during the 1600s.[4] Up until that time, the story most Europeans told themselves—the core story of European culture and politics—was that the social order was ordained by God, who had created a great chain of being, stretching from divinely ordained rulers through lesser monarchs down through the landed aristocracy to peasants and serfs.

Then Thomas Hobbes came along, during a time of social, economic, and political turmoil in England, to argue against that great-chain-of-being story and propose what became the modern conservative story. In his book *Leviathan,* Hobbes suggested that all men were equal, and he argued in favor of private property— two views later also embraced by liberals (and ultimately extended to women and to non-European peoples).

Unlike the liberals who would come later, however, Hobbes believed that because all people are equal, all people are equally dangerous. He believed that human nature was essentially evil and that, left to our own devices, we humans would constantly be engaged in war with one another.

The first truly articulate definer of what has become modern American conservative thought, Hobbes was the mathematics tutor to Charles II during the young prince's exile after the murder of his father; it was during that time that Hobbes wrote and published *Leviathan,* which both defined his view of how civilization came about and also subtly rationalized placing Charles II on the throne.

In the introduction Hobbes told how he was setting out to basically answer the questions *Who are we?* and *Why do we have society?* and *What is the true nature of man?* Civilization, he believed, was the recent, artificial, and clever invention of modern man, and prior to its existence there had been nothing but fear that held humans together.[5]

Hobbes then proceeded to lay out what has become the basis of today's modern conservative worldview and also to lay the foundations for today's modern liberal worldview, which would follow him by about a generation. First, he suggested that the divine right of kings was dead and that therefore no man had an inherent right to rule over another.[6]

This notion of equality was radical stuff for his time and was embraced by the people of England, paving the way for Hobbes's protégé, Charles II, to assume the throne and share power with Parliament.

But Hobbes saw his vision of human equality as a curse, leading to the miserable "natural" state of mankind.[7]

Thus, in Hobbes's mind, the natural state of humankind was to be at war, and peace was merely the absence of war. "From Equality Proceeds Diffidence," Hobbes said, and from diffidence, war. As a result of this, there *must* be, in Hobbes's mind, "allowed" a power of "dominion over men" or else continuous war would always be the result.[8]

This means, Hobbes said, that warfare between men, between families, between states, and between nations is as natural as the weather. It's the normal state of things because humans are, at their core, evil and selfish beings willing to kill one another simply because it's what men do.[9]

This logic, then, led to Hobbes's most famous core assumption, which is absolutely at the heart of modern conservative thinking (and is often quoted in books on conservative philosophy):

> In such condition [without people being ruled by the iron fist of Church or King], there is no place for Industry; because the fruit thereof is uncertain; and consequently no Culture of the Earth; no Navigation, nor use of the commodities that may be imported by Sea; no commodious Building; no Instruments of moving, and removing such things as require much force; no Knowledge of the face of the Earth; no account of Time; no Arts; no Letters; no Society; and which is worst of all, continuall feare, and danger of violent death; And the life of man, solitary, poore, nasty, brutish, and short.

Hobbes was also quite certain that he could see the truth of this in the natives living on the American continent, although he had never visited it or met any of them.[10]

Even today most modern American conservatives believe—wrongly, in the opinion of liberals and most anthropologists—that all American Indian tribes lived in a state of constant hate and warfare against each other before the arrival of the "civilizing" Europeans. On the other hand, most modern American liberals will assert that the majority of American Indian tribes lived in relative peace and harmony both among and between each other and that tribal conflict was the exception brought about mostly by changes in climate from generation to generation.

Conservatives, believing Hobbes's view of human nature to be inviolable, cannot conceive of the possibility that civilizations can exist without constant warfare or an iron-fisted Church or State to prevent that warfare. This is the original modern conservative story. Conservatives believe in what Riane Eisler and others have called the *dominator culture*.[11] They believe that human nature must be dominated for human societies to flourish because without constraint by domination the essentially evil nature of humans will emerge and society will dissolve into chaos.

Conservatives believe that government must be restrained and controlled precisely because it's made up of flawed human beings, "the governed." This is why they're willing to allow corporations to take powers—like controlling our health-care system—that they would never allow to government. Corporations are essentially independent entities and totally without morality (and, thus, without immorality or evil). Being amoral they're less dangerous in the conservative mind than a government controlled by humans, particularly the vast majority of people (whom John Adams called "the rabble") because those people are, at their core, evil.

The conservatives' core belief is that if our essential (evil) human nature is not restrained by *something*—God or priests or corporate bosses—harm will come to society. This is why conservative morality is nearly always focused on restraining individual behavior, particularly private behavior (*With whom are you having sex and in what positions or ways? What are you smoking, drinking, or snorting? Is there a fetus growing inside of you?*). And why they're enthusiastic to "privatize" functions of government, taking the commons out of the hands of We the (evil) People and putting it into the hands of morality-neutral corporations that, in their minds, answer only to a mechanistic and morally neutral "free market."

THE EMERGENCE OF THE MODERN LIBERAL WORLDVIEW

Thomas Hobbes's student Charles II lived to rule for only three years and was replaced by his brother, James II, who was such a maniacal power-freak (and a Catholic in an increasingly Protestant nation) that the people of England rose up and overthrew him in the nearly bloodless "Glorious Revolution" of 1688. But before they would let William and Mary rule, Parliament passed the first real British "bill of rights."

This was the beginning of true democracy in England, and its greatest philosopher was John Locke. His *Two Treatises on Government* was written in part as a rebuttal to Thomas Hobbes. In it Locke laid out the idea that natural law is real, that it doesn't require a state of war, and that one of the goals of civil society should be to know natural law and reflect it in manmade laws.[12]

Locke first developed the idea of private property as being the result of human interaction with nature. A tree is part of the commons, but if part of that tree is worked by a human hand, some of the person is invested in it and the resulting ax handle (or whatever is made) is now the private property of the person who invested it with his human labor. Prior to the introduction of imperishable forms of representative wealth (money), Locke said that natural law forbade any man to accumulate more than he could use. With the introduction of money, however, it was possible for people to accumulate well in excess of what they could use, and Locke suggested it was then up to society (government) to determine what the limits on this accumulation might be.

Thomas Jefferson drew heavily on John Locke's theories. Locke wrote:

> Man being born, as has been proved, with a title to perfect freedom, and an uncontrouled enjoyment of all the rights and privileges of the *law of nature,* equally with any other man, or number of men in the world, *hath by nature a power,* not only to preserve his property, that is, *his life, liberty and estate,* against the injuries and attempts of other men… (emphasis added)

As Thomas Jefferson noted in his *Autobiography,* the genesis of the Declaration of Independence was in the perversion of the tax laws by the transnational corporation the East India Company in getting a huge tax break from the British Parliament so it could destroy the smaller American entrepreneurs and corner the market in tea and other commodities. After the colonists, in the early winter of 1773, threw overboard more than 300 chests of tea in Boston harbor—what would be worth more than $1 million in today's U.S. currency—the British passed the Boston Ports Act that demanded the colonists repay the East India Company for its losses from this illegal act of vandalism and rebellion or the Port of Boston would be closed to further traffic.[13]

This led to some general rabble-rousing on the part of the Founders, with Jefferson writing *A Summary View of the Rights of British America,* which didn't completely call for separation from England but was philosophically moving in that direction. This was followed by Jefferson's writing a "draught of instructions" in how a colony may secede. Most quickly embraced it, although some were only marginally interested.

Ultimately, the process led directly to Jefferson's writing the first draft of the Declaration of Independence, wherein he changed Locke's "life, liberty and estate" to:

> We hold these truths to be self-evident, that all men are created equal, that they are endowed by their Creator with certain unalienable Rights, that among these are Life, Liberty and the

pursuit of Happiness. — That to secure these rights, Governments are instituted among Men, deriving their just powers from the consent of the governed…

This substitution of *happiness* for Locke's language for private property was no accident on Jefferson's part. The core division between Hobbes and Locke, between Sir Edmund Burke and Thomas Jefferson, between conservative and liberal in the 1770s was the theory of the true core of human nature. The majority of the Founders were Lockean liberals, while most of England still held to Hobbesian conservative principles.

Jefferson and other American liberals early on embraced Locke's notion of private property as being essential to liberty, but Jefferson also saw in the issue that Locke wouldn't follow to its conclusion—the unlimited amassment of private property through the accumulation of monetary wealth—a fundamental danger to the public good. By inserting *happiness* instead of *estate*, Jefferson was pointing again to his belief (and that of his peers among the Founders) in the essential goodness of human nature, of happiness as its "original state," and that natural law traced itself back to ensuring happiness as much as it did life and liberty.

To the proto-conservative Hobbes, freedom was found in the restraint of human nature by the iron fist of Church or State, thus preventing the original state of perpetual warfare. To the proto-liberal Locke, freedom was found in the restraint of Church or State, leaving the individual and a self-governing society to reclaim the original state of balance and harmony (and, Jefferson would add, happiness).

To this day, this is still the fundamental cleavage between conservatives and liberals.

Liberals speak of using government for positive ends, but they don't mean to further restrain people. Instead liberals believe that the role of government is to provide a framework within which individuals can achieve their maximum potential.

The closer we can all come to our true human nature, the better, liberals believe. Instead of restraining human nature, liberals want to promote it.

What should be restrained, in the liberal worldview, are those amoral institutions—like corporations—that serve to lock humans into particular social and/or economic roles that prevent both individual and societal self-actualization and achievement of our essential human nature (Jefferson's *happiness*).

This is why liberal morality is nearly always focused on providing for the needs of individuals within society—and was so well articulated by Jesus in the Beatitudes and Matthew 25 when He said, essentially, that we couldn't claim morality if there were hungry, homeless, sick, thirsty, or imprisoned people among us whose needs were not being met.

The fundamental difference between liberals and conservatives is that conservatives think amoral institutions like corporations, or moral institutions like churches, are morally *superior* to immoral/evil humans, and so constraints on governments run by immoral/evil human voters should come from religion and the power of the supposedly amoral marketplace.

Liberals, on the other hand, believe that amoral institutions like corporations and corruptible institutions like churches are *inferior* to moral/good humans, and so want constraints on government to come from the voters/citizens themselves, anchored in the core concepts of human rights and human needs.

The liberal story of our Founders is told in the Preamble to our Constitution, which lays out six purposes for creating our government. Only one has to do with defense, whereas the other five are all about helping our citizens realize their maximum potential:

> We the people of the United States, in order to *form a more perfect union,* establish *justice,* insure domestic *tranquility,* provide for the common *defense,* promote the general *welfare,* and secure the *blessings of liberty* to ourselves and our posterity, do

ordain and establish this Constitution for the United States of America. (emphasis added)

Together, the Declaration of Independence and the Constitution of the United States lay out a clear and solid story of the original worldview of the Founders of our nation, nearly all of them liberal "children of the Enlightenment."

THE ISSUES PLAYLIST: THREE EXAMPLES

Every issue on the political playlist can be told using either the liberal story or the conservative story but is nevertheless grounded in the core good/evil humanity stories just outlined. Here are some examples:

Social Security

Liberals tell a story about each person paying into an insurance system so that we collectively, as a society, can make sure that each of us has enough if the vicissitudes of life strike us, whether those are disability, loss, or old age. Social Security becomes the prime example of the kind of story of a cooperative society that liberals envision and feel is essential for "Life, Liberty and the pursuit of Happiness."

Conservative ideologues first ignore that one-third of Social Security recipients are not retired people but, literally, widows, orphans, and the severely disabled poor. They then tell a story about each person needing to be responsible for investing in their personal future. We deserve to have a good retirement, they suggest, only if we have been "good people" and adopted internal restraints on ourselves and saved for our own futures. If we are without those restraints, the government shouldn't "bail us out."

Unions

Liberals believe that people are most productive when they can realize their potential, so they favor situations like unionization in which workers are on equal footing with bosses so

they can negotiate issues and work out common solutions
to problems. To liberals, unions are a form of democracy
in the workplace, which would otherwise be organized
like a kingdom.

Conservatives believe that to be productive, workers need
restraints, so they favor giving power in the workplace to
bosses, whose eyes are on productivity and profit, and eliminating the power that's given to workers by laws that protect
the right to unionize.

Global Warming

Liberals believe that we humans are part of a larger whole and
are capable of being a positive force in the world. We created
global warming and that means, ultimately, that we have a
responsibility to resolve it through our democratic institutions
(passing laws to restrain CO_2-producing behaviors, sustain-
ability, and the like). The "free market" may eventually remedy
past harms, but with so much at stake we can't afford to wait
to do something about global warming.

Many conservatives worry about global warming but
believe that the best solution is in the so-called free market,
which they believe to be independent of and thus superior to
human nature. Conservatives believe that people are entirely
self-interested and therefore will keep driving their SUVs and
using their gas furnaces until constrained by market forces
like high prices. Their solution to global warming is to wait
until the situation is so bad that there is enough demand on
corporations within the "free market" to develop products
that pollute less and have reduced energy consumption.
Industry will then develop these products on its own so
long as liberals don't use government to interfere with the
workings of the market.

They Can't Govern If They
Don't Believe in Government

Liberals believe—as stated in the Preamble to the Constitution—that five-sixths of the reasons for the existence of government have to do with helping people achieve their fullest

potential and protecting the common wealth and the common future. This is why during the Great Liberal Era from 1935 until 1981 a huge middle class arose, millions moved from the working poor into the middle class, and infrastructure from schools to roads to dams to the ability to put a man on the moon was built.

Conservatives believe that the fundamental strength of a society comes from and is reflected by the power of its wealthiest individuals and its most powerful institutions. They believe that government power should be weak and limited to restraining people: police, prisons, and armies.

Because conservatives don't believe in government beyond these purposes, when conservative governments are called on to do things other than punish, they will inevitably fail.

Recent and obvious examples include George W. Bush turning the consequences of Hurricane Katrina over to private corporations like Pat Robertson's Operation Blessing, Blackwater USA, and Halliburton; turning the occupation of Iraq—after a quick and successful (albeit illegal) war—over to private corporations like Blackwater and Halliburton; Republicans turning our voting rolls over to private voter-purging companies and our voting systems over to private corporations like Diebold; and a nearly thirty-year record since the conservative Reagan revolution of failure to invest in the infrastructure of schools, hospitals, libraries, colleges, national parks, regulatory agencies, and other public institutions.

CRACKING THE CONSERVATIVE/ LIBERAL CODE

Being liberal or conservative isn't a matter of where you stand on any particular issue. Some conservatives are very concerned about global warming. Some liberals oppose abortion. What makes people conservative or liberal is which story they believe at their core about the true nature of humans.

Conservatives view the world as a dangerous and evil place and believe people to be fundamentally selfish. Humans create institutions to protect us from ourselves by constraining and channeling evil human nature in productive and positive ways. The main purpose of government is to protect, mainly through the instruments of police, prisons, and armies.

Liberals view the world as a natural and harmonious place and believe people to be fundamentally good. The purpose of government, therefore, in addition to protecting us from the occasional nutcase, is to help us all achieve our highest potential by providing things that will expand education, skills, and economic opportunities.

After September 11, 2001, George W. Bush was able to use the communication code to persuade many liberals to temporarily believe the conservative story. He used the communication code so effectively he was able to convince Americans that Saddam Hussein, a secular nationalist, was personally connected to the Islamic fundamentalist jihadists who carried out the 9/11 attacks. Many Americans still believe that.[14]

It's interesting to note that Hobbes was writing in a time of great poverty and upheaval in the England of the 1630s (which was then a third-rate power, its economy eclipsed by the Dutch and Spanish trading companies until the mid-1600s, when the British East India Company began successfully competing worldwide). He noted how poverty makes people desperate, and desperate people can be dangerous people. London was filled with them. And he assumed that such poverty and "criminal" behavior was the norm of all societies that preceded "civilization."

Locke, on the other hand, was writing as the East India Company and British colonialism were having considerable economic successes, the Enlightenment was taking hold, and a more substantial middle class was emerging in England. He looked at the behavior of London's emerging middle class as a more accurate reflection of the "natural" state of humanity.

Conservatives may well be right about the "true nature" of people—when they're desperate. Liberals may well be right about the "true nature" of people—when their basic needs are met and they feel safe and secure.

The history of social interaction—from tribal times to civilization to today—has been about providing safety and security, sometimes more successfully than at other times.

Whereas safe, secure people do creative and positive things, desperate people do desperate things.

Before the United States invaded Iraq, there had never, in the seven-thousand-year history of that nation, been a recorded incident of a suicide bomber killing random civilians. After a year of sporadic electricity, no clean water, constant strife, and the heavy foot of a foreign occupier, suicide bombers suddenly became relatively common in Iraq.

One lesson of this has to do with the importance of liberal civil society to maintain democracy, and of democracy to maintain a liberal civil society.

But war is not a form of civility; it's the ultimate failure of civility. Because it is legalized mass murder, it is rightly relegated to the measure of last resort by civilized people the world over. Thus the majority of the civilized world was horrified when the United States launched a preemptive war on Iraq without the authorization of the United Nations.

Yet many Americans bought the initial sales pitch for the war, even as the rest of the world looked on with horror. Listen to George W. Bush in the last speech he gave before he invaded Iraq:[15]

> Some citizens wonder, after 11 years of living with this problem [Saddam Hussein], why do we need to confront it now? And there's a reason. We've experienced the horror of September the 11th. We have seen that those who hate America are willing to crash airplanes into buildings full of innocent people. Our enemies would be no less willing, in fact, they would be eager, to use biological or chemical, or a nuclear weapon.

> Knowing these realities, America must not ignore the threat
> gathering against us. Facing clear evidence of peril, we cannot
> wait for the final proof—the smoking gun—that could come in
> the form of a mushroom cloud.

This speech uses many of the tools and techniques you will
learn in this book. It's pretty clear that Bush is pushing the panic
button, appealing (much like Goosalini) directly to our very primitive fight-or-flight reaction. Less obviously, he's using language
designed to engage our three most basic senses: *seeing, hearing,*
and *feeling.* He's also using even more-subtle hypnotic techniques
here, such as *future pacing,* to create a kind of trance state that will
make us more likely to agree with him.

The communication techniques Bush used to persuade us
to go to war in Iraq are not evil in themselves; they are value-
neutral. Franklin D. Roosevelt used the communication code to
push through the New Deal. Lincoln used the code to motivate
soldiers to win the Civil War and end slavery.

Yet when Lincoln and FDR used the communication code to
push through an idea, their story stuck because it was fundamentally honest. Bush's story wasn't honest, and ultimately it didn't stick.

The difference between Bush and Lincoln, and between
Bush and FDR, is simple and has nothing to do with conserva-
tive/liberal: Bush lied. There was no smoking gun. Bush persuaded
the American people to invade Iraq by motivating them to avoid
"the threat gathering against us" when there was no immediate
threat—at least not from Saddam, as Hans Blix was telling the
United Nations as recently as a week before our invasion of Iraq.
Bush failed what I call the *ecology check*—and it ultimately came
back to bite him.

ECOLOGY CHECKS

When Bush lied about the connection between Saddam Hussein
and al-Qaeda, and lied again about the presence of nuclear weapons

in Iraq, he probably thought the ends justified the means. When he used the communication code to tell those lies, he must have thought the war he was creating was really worth its cost in blood, money, and national prestige.

In politics, as in nature, the most ecological efforts at enhancing social good cause no harm. That's an example of an ecology check.

The word *ecology* means a system in balance. When you are communicating about a particular topic, ask yourself these questions:

■ Does it serve you and others well?

■ Will it help serve community, democracy, and all life on Earth?

■ Is it sustainable over time in a healthy balance?

Because conservatives believe that the natural human role is to dominate all of nature and, ultimately, each other (to prevent nature's evil and our evil from emerging), they sometimes will justify using whatever means necessary to bring the undisciplined public into line. Similarly, sometimes liberals have used deceit or raw power to bring about what they think are the solutions to greater social ills. These are both examples of failed ecology checks.

Fear is created about a group—be it communists, gays, hippies, the Japanese during World War II, or members of another religion—and in the short term there is a strong and immediate response. We human beings, like other animals, are hardwired to move away from anything dangerous.

Over the past few decades in particular, some politicians have become very competent at using fear to paint a larger and more systemic picture of a reality that is always dangerous. This picture gives them power because it is based in a very powerful, primitive emotion and it emerges from their essential frame of reality.

Franklin D. Roosevelt became president during the Great Depression at a time when everyone was terrified of the future.

But he said, literally, "We have nothing to fear but fear itself," and that positive message helped pull the American people together to bring our economy and society back on track.

To help you crack the communication code for yourself, I'll show you, tell you, and hand you the tools you need to understand how people think, sort, and understand the world. Along the way we'll examine how the communication code can be used to frame, explain, and promote or oppose issues that face the United States and the world—with examples to help you see and learn the stories of the traditional progressive values that made America great.

As you read deeply into this book, you'll see things you hadn't realized were right there in front of you all along in everything from advertising to political rants. You'll discover resources and personal abilities within yourself and find out how they can be used.

You'll become an agent of change, in the finest tradition of those brilliant and unconsciously competent geniuses Thomas Paine, Thomas Jefferson, and the cousins Roosevelt.

CHAPTER 2

CRACKING THE STORY CODE

Words are, of course, the most powerful drug used by mankind.

— RUDYARD KIPLING

Before we wrote things down, we told stories. Aboriginal and indigenous people have elaborate and detailed stories about *everything* in their world, and those stories code information both for the things and for the culture.

The classic model of a story builds emotional impact in five stages around the story's core message:

■ Typically, a story starts out with a character having his or her world thrown out of balance.

■ Then there's a series of progressive complications as she struggles to get her life back into balance.

■ Next she's confronted with a crisis—a choice she must make that will forever change her world.

■ This is followed by the climax of the story—making the choice and experiencing the result—and this is where both the moral/message of the story as well as its maximum emotional impact are coded.

■ Then the story resolves, with loose ends being tied up and everybody living "happily ever after."

This five-part story structure is so hardwired into humanity that you find it in 50,000-year-old Australian Aboriginal stories, 40,000-year-old stories from the San Bushmen of the Kalahari, and 20,000-year-old stories from American Indian communities. You find it everywhere—from the works of Gilgamesh to Shakespeare to Steinbeck to Spielberg.

Because storytelling is so powerful and so memorable and can pack such an emotional punch, if you want people to learn something, wrap it up in a story and it'll last years longer in their minds than if you simply gave them information.

Consider, for example, a story I first learned from a talk I heard about a decade ago in Vermont by an Abenaki American Indian storyteller named Jesse Bruchac. His telling of the story was far richer and more complex than the version I'm sharing here with you from an old memory, but hopefully mine will serve to illustrate the point of this section.

A little boy was walking through the woods one day and found a magic stick. He picked it up and thought, *I can do anything now! I can change the world!* He continued to walk, and when he looked up next he wasn't sure where he was.

Getting lost in the woods is a very big problem, thought the boy. *If I always knew which direction north was, whether it was cloudy or sunny, light or dark, I could always find my way home—and so could all the other little boys wandering through the forest.* As he had these thoughts, he saw some squirrels. He waved the stick and said, "Let all the squirrels' tails point north." And they did!

That's good, thought the boy. *Now I and all the other little boys who need to walk in the woods will never get lost.* And he walked along, whistling, quite satisfied with himself.

But the squirrels were not very happy. As they chattered with each other over what to do next, in the squirrel way, a skunk walked by and asked, "What happened to your tails?"

The squirrels replied, "A little boy waved his magic stick and now all our tails are pointed to the north."

"That wasn't very polite," said the skunk.

So the skunk took a shortcut and got ahead of the boy on his way through the forest. The boy saw him and, knowing about skunks, knew that you have nothing to fear if you don't try to hurt them. "Hello, Mr. Skunk," the boy said. "How are you this fine day?"

The skunk said, "Are you the boy who made the tails of the squirrels point north?"

"Yes," said the boy, swelling his chest out with pride. "And now no little boy will ever get lost!"

"Well," said the skunk, "I don't think that was very considerate or wise. Perhaps you would like *me* to point *my* tail to the north, too." And with that, he turned around, lifted his tail, and sprayed the boy from head to toe.

In those days American Indians well knew that only an idiot gets squirted by a skunk. The boy knew that when he got home, all of his friends would laugh at him. He'd have to roll in mud and sleep outside the village for three days until the smell went away, and that's both uncomfortable and humiliating.

At first, as the boy continued walking down the trail, his nose and eyes stinging and his skin tingling, he felt sorry for himself and angry at the skunk. *Why did he do that?* the boy thought. *I didn't threaten or harm him!* But as he kept walking, he considered the skunk's words and realized that he really had no right to change the tails of the squirrels just to make life easier for him and other little boys.

As this realization struck him, he looked at his magic stick with a newfound concern, and then waved it and said, "All the squirrels' tails will go back to normal." Then he dug a deep hole and buried the stick so thoroughly and carefully that even he would never find it again, and he went off to roll in the mud.

The obvious moral of the story is that the means do not justify the ends. But the story also contains a number of culturally important pieces of information for the Abenaki.

One is about Mother Nature and how we interfere with nature at our own peril, particularly with the "magic stick" of our large brains. We live in an interconnected world in which making even one seemingly small change will ultimately have an impact on everything else.

Another is about how and how not to interact with a skunk and other animals.

Another is about the vital importance of knowing which way north is. In the original telling, there were far more details about squirrels, about some of the trees, and about the history of magic. All were ways of passing culture down from generation to generation—always embedded in story so it would be accurately remembered.

Even literate societies do this. Consider the story of the boy who cried wolf, which uses the traditional five-part story structure to embed the message about the importance of alarming people only when there's a genuine reason to do so. Or consider the story "The Emperor's New Clothes" and the child who had the courage to point out that the king was naked—carrying the cultural story of the importance of speaking truth to power. Even some of our dysfunctional stories persist—like Cinderella, which tells women that their place is to be maids and their salvation is to find a rich man with a foot fetish.

Stories are powerful. If you want people to understand your point, and to remember it for a long time, embed the information in a story.

PART II

FEELING
COMES FIRST

CHAPTER 3

CRACKING THE SENSORY CODE

When people talk, listen completely. Most people never listen.

— ERNEST HEMINGWAY

I do talk radio, and because my aim is to encourage debate (and when appropriate, change people's minds), I tend to invite onto my radio program many people with whom I disagree. To turn this collision of opposing views into an interesting conversation instead of a one-sided rant, however, I have to first establish a rapport with my guest. First I try to find common ground. For example, conservative or liberal, we both love this country. We both live in this country. We both want a better world for our children and grandchildren. We all want safety and security.

Staying at the level of generalities usually doesn't work for long, however, because even at that level conservatives and liberals are telling themselves different stories about how the world is and how it should be. Conservatives, who believe that people are evil and need their natural impulses restrained by being channeled into productive behavior, love our country because it is based on free-market capitalism, which they believe rewards those who work the hardest. Liberals, who believe that people are good and need opportunities to develop their potential, love our country because it is based on a form of democratic government that posits life, liberty, and the pursuit of happiness as our most cherished values. It doesn't take long for liberals and conservatives to start talking past each other.

If you really want to establish rapport with someone, first step into their world.

To get to the building blocks that make up a person's fundamental story about the world, we listen to how they speak and thus begin to understand how they think.

Listen long enough and you'll discover that communication begins with the senses.

We talk about the world in pretty much the same way that we experience it.

Here's an example from my family. A few Christmases ago, my wife and I were fortunate enough to have all three of our adult kids with us, and we decided to all go to a movie. We had spread the newspaper out on the table, turned to the movie pages, and were trying to decide which movie to go to.

My visually oriented wife, Louise, said, "Well, let's see which movie we should go see."

One of our daughters, also very visual, immediately replied, "Well, I'd like to go see that one," and she pointed to a particular movie ad.

We kept talking, and we all noticed that our son hadn't made a suggestion. So we asked him, "Which movie do you want to go to?"

He said, "I'm not really sure."

So our first daughter asked, "Well, which one looks best to you?"

And he answered, "I don't know."

Then our second daughter, who's very auditory (like me), asked, "Well, which one sounds best to you?"

Again, he answered, "I don't know."

All of a sudden I realized what was going on and so I said to him, "Which one feels right to you?"

And he said, "Well, that one!" and pointed to one of the movies.

All along my son knew what he felt, but he couldn't explain it in a visual sense or an auditory sense in response to visually or auditorily based questions. This is very common. We experience the world through our senses. If we were unable to see, to hear, to feel, to notice balance, to smell, and to taste, we would have no experience of the world's existence. All internal experience begins as some sort of external experience that we then internalize.

What's critical to deciphering communication is to realize that we all have different ways of encoding and storing and using that information. My son didn't understand the rest of the family's questions because he experiences the world primarily through feeling things rather than hearing or seeing them. Most people rely primarily on one of our sensory systems and use that system as their main way of experiencing the world.

These senses, like the rest of the communication code, are value-neutral. Someone who is visually oriented can be conservative or liberal. That's useful. It means that once you identify someone's primary way of experiencing the world, you can use that tool to communicate with them at a very basic level even if you don't share the same story about the meaning of the world.

MODALITIES

People in the communication field refer to sensory information used in this way as *modalities*. People who primarily *see* the world are using a *visual modality*. People who use their *hearing* to experience the world are using an *auditory modality*. People who *feel* the world are using what is called a *kinesthetic modality*.

We can usually use all of these sensory modalities when we need to, but most of us have one primary modality that acts as our first filter. For example, my primary way of knowing the world is auditory. It's probably why I enjoy doing radio. I think it's also why I can write reasonably well and love to read—because that's all auditory: when I'm writing I'm hearing my own voice inside my head going out on the page, and when I'm reading I'm hearing the voices of the author and the characters.

What's Your Primary Sense?

Rank each of the three answer options below between 1 and 3, with 3 being "most often true" and 1 being "least often true." When you're finished, add up all the V's (visual), A's (auditory), and K's (kinesthetic). The numerical scores will tell you (show you? give you a feeling for?) with which of the three representational systems you're most and least familiar. Keep in mind that, at least at this point, this is just for your entertainment:

1. I naturally and easily say things like:
   ___ v "I see what you mean"
   ___ a "That sounds sensible to me"
   ___ k "I have a good feeling about that"

2. When I encounter an old friend, I often say:
   ___ v "It's great to see you again!"
   ___ a "It's great to hear your voice again!"
   ___ k "I've missed you" (and give a big hug)

3. I have:
   ___ v a good eye for décor and color coordination
   ___ a the ability to arrange the stereo and speakers so the music is balanced and sonorous
   ___ k a special feeling for my favorite rooms

4. I let other people know how I'm feeling by:
   ___ v the clothes I wear and the way I do my hair or makeup
   ___ a the tone of my voice, sighs, and other sounds
   ___ k my posture

5. My favorite romantic encounters include:
   ___ v watching the other person, or vivid visualizations or visual fantasy
   ___ a listening to the sounds the other person makes
   ___ k touching and being touched by the other person

6. When I want to totally understand something:

___ v I make pictures of it in my mind

___ a I talk to myself about it

___ k I roll it around until I have a good feeling about it

7. When I'm deciding on an important action, I:

___ v must see all aspects of the situation

___ a must be able to justify the decision to myself and/or somebody else

___ k know when it's the right decision because my gut feelings tell me so

8. When it's important to me to influence another person, I pay careful attention to:

___ v the pictures I paint with my descriptions

___ a the intonation and the pace of my voice

___ k what kind of emotional impact I can bring to the situation

9. When I'm bored, I'm more likely to:

___ v change the way I look or how things around me are arranged

___ a whistle, hum, or play by making sounds in my throat or chest

___ k stretch, exercise, or take a hot bath

10. My favorite authors:

___ v paint vivid pictures of interesting places

___ a write dialogue that sounds true to life

___ k give me a feeling for the story that is moving and meaningful

11. I can tell what others are thinking by:

___ v the look on their face

___ a the tone of their voice

___ k the vibes I get from them

12. When I'm reading a menu, trying to decide what to order, I:
____ v visualize the food
____ A discuss with myself the various options
____ K read the list and choose what feels best

13. I would rather:
____ v look at the pictures in an art gallery
____ A listen to a symphony or a rock concert
____ K participate in a sporting or athletic event

14. When I'm in a bar with a band playing, I find most interesting:
____ v watching the other people or the band
____ A closing my eyes and listening to the music
____ K dancing with or feeling close to the people around me

15. A true statement is:
____ v "It's important how you look if you want to influence others"
____ A "People don't know a thing about you until they've heard what you have to say"
____ K "It takes time to really get in touch with another person's core self"

Total your scores here:
____ v (visual)
____ A (auditory)
____ K (kinesthetic)

Most people in our culture are visual. My wife, Louise, who is very visual, reads about twice as fast as I do. When she's reading, she's making pictures in her mind, but she only rarely sounds out the words in her mind the way I do.

No matter which sensory modality is primary for individuals, they disclose it in the way they think, talk, and write.

Visual people think/experience/talk/write in pictures. A visual person will say, for example: "I see what you're talking about. I now understand—it's crystal clear!" "We need to shine the light of day on this to see it better. Let's show our readers what we mean. Here's how I see this happening." They'll even say on the telephone, when they can't actually see the person to whom they're talking, "I'll see you later."

Auditory people often prefer listening to the radio instead of watching television; they live in a sea of sound. When they communicate, an auditory person will say: "I hear what you're saying. We need to tell this story to as many people as possible so they can all hear it in a meaningful way. Here's how I'd want the message to sound." Auditory people often end phone calls with, "I'll talk with you later."

People whose primary way of understanding is kinesthetic, experience the world through their feelings. When they see and hear things, they translate those visions and stories into feelings. Kinesthetic people will say, "I get your point. Thanks for sharing. I like how you said it, and I want to take it to the next level." They'll often end a phone call with, "I'll catch you later" or "Let's stay in touch."

There are a few of us who have as a primary sensory modality a sense other than seeing, hearing, or feeling. In my fifty-plus years on this planet, I've met two people who leaned heavily on their sense of smell and taste, who remembered events by what they ate there and who described ideas as having "a good flavor" or with similar olfactory or gustatory metaphors. Both of these people had a weight problem, by the way, although that's a pretty small sample on which to draw any conclusions. But such people are rare; most of us are visual, auditory, or kinesthetic.

Psychologist David Lemire found that 75 percent of adult learners in America are primarily visual.[1] Having worked in aboriginal and indigenous societies on five continents, I've found that between 75 and 95 percent of these folks are primarily kinesthetic. Yet when they move from "the reservation" into "the city" and grow up going to "European" schools, they very often become primarily visual or auditory, like the average American. This tells me that kinesthetics represent the "natural" human way of being, probably our most functional and useful way of being, but also a way of being that's changed or distorted by the experience of our public schools and early life, where virtually 100 percent of information is presented either auditorily (teachers lecturing or by reading books) or visually (through metaphor, pictures, and TV).

CRACKING THE MODAL CODE

Sensory modalities are very important for communication because when we process new information, we tend to use our primary sensory system to create internal memory structures describing what the world means and how things are.

For example, when a memorable event like 9/11 occurs, we will each store that memory differently. Even reading those numbers, people who are primarily visual may have flashed to pictures of the towers falling. People who are primarily auditory may remember the sounds of the towers falling, or the screaming and sirens, or a particular newscaster's voice. People who are primarily kinesthetic will remember their shock at hearing the news and the surreal inertia they may have experience for days afterward. The memory is literally stored in our brains through these sensory modalities.

If you want to effectively communicate with someone, it's important to first know which sensory modality is primary for them and then to use that modality to communicate. The key to cracking the modal code is simple once you understand modalities: people tend to communicate using metaphors from their primary modalities. When a kinesthetic person communicates, he does so using metaphors and words based on physical experience, touch, and feelings. For example, when you want to effectively communicate with a kinesthetic person, use language and metaphor that likewise evoke physical experience, touch, and feelings. Similarly, talk in visual metaphor to visually oriented people, and auditory metaphor to auditory folks.

If you want to communicate with a group of people, however, it's useful to craft the message in such a way that it touches all three modalities. You can hear me do that on the radio (or see me do it on this page) by stringing all the modalities together into a sentence.

I'll start out saying, "I want to talk to you today about the stories that we tell ourselves, the way we view the world, and the way we all feel as Americans."

So some visual people in the room are thinking, *I see that.*

Auditory people are saying, "Oh, yeah, I hear that. That makes sense."

And the kinesthetic people say, "Feels good to me."

BECOMING MULTIMODAL

The greatest politicians and the greatest speeches are multimodal. Here are two examples. The first is from Ronald Reagan's famous remarks at the Brandenburg Gate on June 12, 1987. People who have bought into the cult of Reaganism believe these remarks inspired Eastern Europe to tear down the wall just a year and a half later, on November 9, 1989. (The rest of us just looked at the CIA public reports during the previous two decades to see that the Soviet Union was disintegrating from within and its demise had little to do with Reagan. Nonetheless, his speechwriter, Peter

Robinson, wrote a brilliant speech for him to deliver.) Modalities
in the following excerpt are underlined.

Remarks at the Brandenburg Gate
June 12, 1987

Chancellor Kohl, Governing Mayor Diepgen, ladies and gentle-
men: Twenty-four years ago, President John F. Kennedy visited
Berlin, speaking to the people of this city and the world at the
City Hall. Well, since then two other presidents have come, each
in his turn, to Berlin. And today I, myself, make my second visit
to your city.

We come to Berlin, we American presidents, because it's our
duty to speak, in this place, of freedom. But I must confess, we're
drawn here by other things as well: by the feeling of history in
this city, more than 500 years older than our own nation; by the
beauty of the Grunewald and the Tiergarten; most of all, by your
courage and determination. Perhaps the composer Paul Lincke
understood something about American presidents. You see, like
so many presidents before me, I come here today because wherever I go, whatever I do: Ich hab noch einen Koffer in Berlin
[I still have a suitcase in Berlin].

Our gathering today is being broadcast throughout Western
Europe and North America. I understand that it is being seen
and heard as well in the East. To those listening throughout
Eastern Europe, a special word: Although I cannot be with you,
I address my remarks to you just as surely as to those standing
here before me. For I join you, as I join your fellow countrymen
in the West, in this firm, this unalterable belief: Es gibt nur ein
Berlin [There is only one Berlin].

Notice how carefully Peter Robinson layered the modalities
of Reagan's speech. He starts with the auditory and the kinesthetic
because he is, literally, speaking to people and wants to create a
feeling in them. By the middle of the second paragraph, however,
he appeals specifically to visual types who may not be seeing
themselves in his picture.

The third paragraph is a masterpiece of multimodality, with visual, auditory, and kinesthetic references piled upon each other. That is no mistake as this is the moment that Reagan must establish a rapport and tie his belief system to that of his listeners in both West and East Berlin.

Reagan was both a naturally competent communicator and an actor who spent the first part of his life learning how to communicate. Here's an excerpt from the most famous speech by another of the greatest political communicators of our time, Mario Cuomo, who was attempting to unseat Reagan. The speech that the governor of New York gave at the opening of the 1984 Democratic Convention has continued to resonate with Democrats today (showing up most recently in Senator John Edwards's campaign speeches). Once again the modalities are underlined:

> Ten days ago, President Reagan admitted that although some people in this country seemed to be doing well nowadays, others were unhappy, even worried, about themselves, their families, and their futures. The President said that he didn't understand that fear. He said, "Why, this country is a shining city on a hill." And the President is right. In many ways we are a shining city on a hill.

> But the hard truth is that not everyone is sharing in this city's splendor and glory. A shining city is perhaps all the President sees from the portico of the White House and the veranda of his ranch, where everyone seems to be doing well. But there's another city; there's another part to the shining city; the part where some people can't pay their mortgages, and most young people can't afford one; where students can't afford the education they need, and middle-class parents watch the dreams they hold for their children evaporate.

> In this part of the city there are more poor than ever, more families in trouble, more and more people who need help but can't find it. Even worse: There are elderly people who tremble in the basements of the houses there. And there are people who sleep

in the city streets, in the gutter, <u>where the glitter doesn't show</u>. There are ghettos where thousands of young people, without a job or an education, <u>give their lives away</u> to drug dealers every day. <u>There is despair</u>, Mr. President, in the faces <u>that you don't see</u>, <u>in the places that you don't visit</u> in your shining city.

In this speech Cuomo begins with the kinesthetic and the auditory, then moves to the kinesthetic and the visual. His point is that President Reagan does not *see* the pain of the American people. The subtext is that Reagan is operating in only an auditory modality and that this has limited his vision. Cuomo emphasizes what Reagan is missing by staying, through most of the speech, in the visual modality and connecting that visual modality to the kinesthetic—the feelings those visuals evoke.

Toward the end of the speech, however, Cuomo moves back to what should be the president's home ground, the auditory, connecting the auditory with the same feelings previously evoked by the visuals:

Maybe, maybe, Mr. President, if you <u>visited</u> some more places; maybe if you <u>went</u> to Appalachia where some people still live in sheds; maybe if you <u>went</u> to Lackawanna where thousands of unemployed steel workers <u>wonder</u> why we subsidized foreign steel. Maybe—maybe, Mr. President, if you <u>stopped</u> in at a shelter in Chicago and <u>spoke</u> to the homeless there; maybe, Mr. President, if you <u>asked</u> a woman who had been denied the help she needed to <u>feed</u> her children because <u>you said</u> you needed the money for a tax break for a millionaire or for a missile we couldn't afford to use.

Notice that the president is cast as someone who uses only the auditory modality and is blind and unfeeling when it comes to what real Americans see and suffer. Cuomo is suggesting that because the president is limited to one modality, he should use that modality to listen to real Americans rather than to his corporate advisers.

It is this beneath-the-scenes play of sensory modalities—this code—that makes Cuomo's speech so powerful at communicating a fundamental truth. And now you have cracked it.

CHAPTER 4

THE BODY'S SECRET LANGUAGE

And as we let our own light shine, we unconsciously give
other people permission to do the same. As we are liberated
from our fear, our presence automatically liberates others.

— MARIANNE WILLIAMSON

Back in the late 1970s, I was the executive director of a residential treatment facility for abused and emotionally disturbed kids. The psychologist we had hired to help the kids showed me how we could consciously use language to produce unconscious change. I started taking Richard Bandler's classes on communication techniques[1] and eventually became a certified NLP communication trainer.

I discovered that once you decode the way that human beings make decisions—how our neurons fire—you can shape your language to take advantage of that code. The National Security Agency (NSA) knows this code. So does Madison Avenue. (I've done training for both.) And no one has cracked the communication code more effectively than modern Republicans.

Here's an example. You may remember a series of infamous ads that the George Bush Sr. team created during the presidential election of 1988 when he ran against Michael Dukakis. They were what are broadly known today as "the Willie Horton ads."

Dukakis was governor of Massachusetts. He had reduced the unemployment rate in his state from 11 to 4 percent, balanced his state's budget, cut taxes, and improved programs to care for society's most vulnerable and fragile citizens. It was a stellar record, one that anyone familiar with Massachusetts knew was solid. Dukakis believed he could run and win on a campaign of "doing for America what he did for Massachusetts."

Because this was such a powerful political message, the Bush/Quayle team decided to attack Dukakis where he was strongest—on his record as governor of Massachusetts. They combed over the many different things that had happened while Dukakis was governor.

Back in 1972 Republican Massachusetts governor Francis W. Sargent had signed into law a bill that—as part of a more comprehensive program to build rehabilitation into the prison system— allowed some prisoners to have weekend furloughs.

It was still law when Dukakis came into office, and he abolished it on April 28, 1988. Before it was abolished, however, a murderer named Willie Horton had been let out on a weekend furlough and had committed rape and murder.

After letting Dukakis build a strong and recognizable following on the "doing for America what he did for Massachusetts" slogan, the Bush campaign let loose with their secret weapon. On September 21, 1988, three weeks before the general election and half a year after Dukakis had ended the prison furlough program put into place by a previous, Republican governor, they began running the Willie Horton ads.

The first set of ads, created by the Americans for Bush arm of the National Security Political Action Committee, was called "Weekend Passes" and featured a menacing photo of Willie Horton along with a litany of his crimes while on furlough, including "kidnapping, stabbing, and raping."[2]

On October 5, a day after the "Weekend Passes" ad was taken off the airwaves and also the date of the infamous Bentsen-Quayle debate ("You, sir, are no John Kennedy"), the Bush campaign ran its own ad, "Revolving Door."[3] That ad, as described by InsidePolitics .org, told viewers that Dukakis had "vetoed mandatory sentences for drug dealers" and "vetoed the death penalty" while showing images of prison guards at work. Then the ad told viewers, "His revolving door prison policy gave weekend furloughs to first-degree murderers not eligible for parole." The ad showed an image of a revolving door formed by bars, rotating as men in prison uniform walked through, with the message "And Many Are Still at Large" superimposed. Then came the punch line: "Now Michael Dukakis says he wants to do for America what he's done for Massachusetts." (The picture changes to a guard on a roof with a watchtower in the background.) "America can't afford that risk."

This ad didn't mention Willie Horton—but it didn't have to. The "Revolving Door" ad was creating a code that linked the earlier ad that used the same visual and auditory techniques and named Willie Horton, rapist and murderer, to the small color picture of Michael Dukakis and his signature phrase that he wanted to do for America what he had done for Massachusetts.

Notice what happened. Reality no longer mattered (that Dukakis had already ended the program—or that a Republican governor had started it—wasn't even reported in most of the mainstream corporate media, although they did cover the ad at length). The content delivery—with its unconscious reminder of the fear elicited by Willie Horton—overrode the content itself.

It didn't matter that Dukakis had reduced the unemployment rate in his state from 11 to 4 percent, or that he did that while balancing the budget, cutting taxes, and taking care of society's most vulnerable and fragile citizens.[4] What Mike Dukakis had done, what he stood for, what he said, didn't matter because when people saw and heard those Bush team ads, all they felt was fear.

As Dukakis's campaign manager, Susan Estrich,[5] said: "The symbolism was very powerful...you can't find a stronger metaphor, intended or not, for racial hatred in this country than a Black

man raping a White woman....I talked to people afterward....
Women said they couldn't help it, but it scared the living daylights
out of them."

For the last two weeks of the campaign, whenever Dukakis
used his signature phrase, people recoiled in fear. Politically, he
was as dead as Willie Horton's victims.

FEELING COMES BEFORE THINKING

When we communicate with each other, we often believe we are
using the most rational parts of our minds. We think we know
exactly why we say something in a certain way. We think we know
what someone else is saying to us.

But we humans, being the product of a long evolutionary
process, really have three brains. And politicians who win campaigns do so because they speak to all three of those brains.

First there's the most primitive of our brains, sometimes referred to as the "reptilian brain" because we share it in common
with reptiles like alligators and komodo dragons. The reptilian
brain has a singular focus: survival. It doesn't think in abstract
terms, and it doesn't feel complex emotions. Instead, it's responsible for fight or flight, hunger and fear, attack or run. It's also nonverbal—you can stimulate it with the right words, but it operates
purely at the level of visceral stimulus/response.

The second brain is one we share with the animals that came
along after reptiles: mammals. The "mammalian brain"—sometimes referred to as the "limbic brain" because it extends around
and off of the reptilian brain in a dog-leg shape that resembles a
limb—handles complex emotions like love, indignation, compassion, envy, and hope. Anybody who has worked with animals or
had a pet knows that mammals share these emotions with humans
because we share this brain. Although a snake can't feel shame or
enthusiasm, it's completely natural for a dog or cat. And, like the
reptilian brain, the mammalian brain can be stimulated indirectly

by words and is also nonverbal. It expresses itself exclusively in the form of feelings, most often felt in the heart or the gut.

The third brain—the neocortex ("new" cortex)—is something we share with the higher apes, although ours is a bit more sophisticated. Resting over the limbic brain (which is atop the reptilian brain), our neocortex is where we process abstract thought, words and symbols, logic, and time.

Recent research has shown that the brain creates information as well as processes it. A study published in 2005 demonstrated that the brain uses the same exact mechanism to perceive a smile and to create a smile.[6] This is pure biology—our senses detect a smile and our brain replicates it.

Does that mean we are just machines? No. In a way scientists are just beginning to understand, these biological processes are also related to our feelings. When we see a smile, and when we smile back, we actually feel happier. Actually, anytime we smile, we feel happier. The leading psychologist of human emotion, Dr. Robert Zajonc, has shown that simply smiling can make you feel happy.[7]

This is a very deep part of the communication code. Above and beyond all the amazing things we do, we humans are still animals, and our communication is tied to our biology. We react to sensations. That is why the primary modalities of truly effective communication all are based on the senses. And within these modalities are submodalities that drill down even deeper into the brain.

How Feelings Affect Communication

Since René Descartes, many in the Western world have believed, *I think, therefore I am.* We prioritize thinking. That point of view has led to some very important achievements. Some would say that America would not be a democracy today if the Founders hadn't believed they could rationally determine the very best system of governance.

Rationality was at the core of our nation's founding. One of the essential differences between the conservative and the liberal worldview is that liberals believe in rationality whereas conservatives believe that human events are ordered by forces that are beyond the ability of our rational mind to understand or control. (This belief in rationality was so strong among the Founders that Thomas Jefferson even took the first four books of the New Testament—the four Gospels that tell the stories of Jesus—and cut out of them all supernatural events. What he strung back together were largely the words and the nonmiraculous deeds of Jesus, and Jefferson's handiwork has been continuously in print for more than two hundred as *The Jefferson Bible.*)

Yet even for the most stolid believers in rationality, the reality is that when we are making the most important life decisions, we almost always base them on our feelings rather than our rational thoughts. Some people call these feelings their "gut" or "intuition." Some people who are as rational as Jefferson like to call them "rational certainties." Call them what you will; the decisions we make are based in small or large part on feelings.

Science, that most rational of endeavors, has finally acknowledged that feelings precede thinking. In a groundbreaking work published in 1980 in *American Psychologist,* the journal of the American Psychological Association, Dr. Robert Zajonc argued persuasively that decision-making is based on our feelings.[8]

Zajonc points out that we can "like something or be afraid of it before we know precisely what it is and perhaps even without knowing what it is." That's because we "think" first through the limbic brain. Zajonc writes, "The limbic system that controls emotional reactions was there before we evolved language and our present form of thinking." He continues, "It is rather...likely that the affective system retained its autonomy," remaining separate from cognition. That means our ways of feeling precede and are different and separate from our ways of thinking.

Our five senses transmit sensory data directly to the reptilian brain, which translates the data into our most primitive forms of emotion. Those data are then transferred to the higher limbic and cortical brains. *We feel before we even have a chance to think.* What that means for communication is that the most effective communicators rely on feeling-based (kinesthetic) communicative strategies. They reach people at the level of the limbic brain, at the seat of feeling.

THE SUBMODALITIES CODE

The communication code for our feelings is based in the sensory modalities. But within the primary modalities are submodalities that allow us to fine-tune and direct our specific impact and message toward the limbic brain.

Auditory submodalities have to do with how we hear. Do you hear the idea or event behind you? Do you hear it in front of you? Is it loud or soft, distant or far, clear or muffled?

Kinesthetic submodalities have to do with where we experience our feelings in our bodies (there is always a physical corollary to kinesthetic content) and how we feel them. Our language reveals that we often feel ideas in parts of our body: "He felt that like a hot poker to the leg"; "He felt punched in the gut"; "Her heart raced."

Visual submodalities have to do with how we see an idea or event. Is it big or small? Near or far? Bright or dim? Color or black-and-white? Still picture or a movie? Crystal clear or fuzzy?

Submodalities are the ways our brain sorts sensory information. Sensory information does not come in through the rational part of our brain, the left hemisphere, the part that is logical, the part that does quadratic equations. Instead, all the information we gather about the world comes in through our sensory reptilian and limbic brains; it is first processed, mostly in the irrational and nonspeaking right hemisphere of our neocortex.

We have experiences throughout the day; we see things, hear things, feel things. We have to figure out a way to make sense of and to store and save those experiences as memories. Throughout the course of the day, we write many of them down on a little one-day scratchpad in the reptilian brain called the *hippocampus.*

Then at night, as we dream, we process that information, which is one reason why our dreams seem irrational: we're trying to figure out, *Okay, what happened today that I need to store and what do I need to throw away?* We attach emotional tags to ideas and events that we need to store. We store information by emotion.

Imagine that the mind's filing system is like the Pentaflex office filing system. Imagine your mind is filled with colored folders—blue, yellow, red, each representing an emotion; then inside those folders you can put the smaller manila file folders representing specific event memories. Speaking metaphorically, the big colored folders encode or sort and store information by emotions. There's a yellow folder for happiness, a green for love, and a red folder for anger, and each folder is very subtle. There are thousands of variations of emotion for which we don't even have words: these are the many colored folders. And inside of those are the smaller manila folders made up of the individual experiences.

The way the larger, colored folders are organized is by submodality. Submodalities are the labels that define not only where the memories are but also how they exist.

Here's how we crack the communication code: because we actually understand the world through these submodalities, you can use them to change how you—and others—feel and thus how we (or they) think.

CREATING A POLITICAL SCALPEL

You can actually change how someone feels about past events or ideas by helping them change their "locations" in their sorting system.

If your listener is willing, you can actually change how he thinks about an event in just a few minutes by asking him to refile the experience under a different submodality. If he sees his experience in color, change it to black-and-white. If he sees it close up, ask him to push it farther away. If he feels it as cold, ask him to make it feel hot.

CHANGING SUBMODALITIES

A Transcript from the Thom Hartmann Program
December 15, 2006

After describing how submodalities work, I asked for volunteers to call in who would be okay with my changing one of their memories on the air, using the submodality filing system. The first volunteer was Barbara, listening in Los Angeles.

THOM: Hi, Barbara! Thanks for calling in. What I'd like you to do is remember something in the recent past, the last week or so, that was a moderately unpleasant experience. The example that I would give is like somebody flipping you off in traffic or a surly waiter.

BARBARA: Yeah, I got one.

THOM: You got one, okay, great. Now I want you to describe to me the submodalities associated with it. In other words, when you remember that experience, and you see the picture of that, do you see the picture in color or black-and-white?

BARBARA: Color.

THOM: Okay. Describe in space where it is: in front of you, behind you, you know, where is it?… Is it like 5 feet in front of you, is it 20 feet behind you, is it 6 feet off to your left?

BARBARA: In front of me.

THOM: It's in front of you. And how far away?

BARBARA: I would say 10, 5 feet.

THOM: 5 feet. Okay. Is there sound associated with it?

BARBARA: Yeah, there's sound.

THOM: Okay. And is it a movie or is it a still picture?

BARBARA: It's a movie picture.

THOM: Okay, great. So, what I'd like you to do, Barbara, is first of all push that picture, so we figured out some of the submodalities associated with it, right?

BARBARA: Yeah.

THOM: What I'd like you to do is push that picture about twice as far away from you. Push it like 10, 15, 20 feet away from you first of all.

BARBARA: Okay. I've done it.

THOM: Okay, and now turn it black-and-white.

BARBARA: Okay. But that's hard. That's hard, to turn it into black-and-white.

THOM: Oh, interesting. Okay, well you can leave it color if you want. Maybe your brain doesn't want it black-and-white yet.

BARBARA: No, my brain doesn't want black-and-white.

THOM: Okay, well that's cool. Leave it as color. I want you to scroll all the way to the end of the movie and freeze-frame it…

BARBARA: Freeze-frame it, okay.

THOM: And now, in just a second I'm going to make a *whoosh* sound and I'm going to ask you to play it backward; and you know how you play a movie backward, everybody moves like in the old Charlie Chaplin movies and everybody talks backward like Donald Duck. And I want you to right now play it backward all the way back to the beginning with everybody going, everything going backward—*whoosh.* Like that.

BARBARA: Yep. Yep, I did.

THOM: Okay, all the way to the beginning. Now freeze-frame it at the beginning; and do you see yourself in the picture or do you see it as if you were there?

BARBARA: I see myself in the picture.

THOM: Okay, great. What I'd like you to do is I'd like you to paint rainbows across that picture now and put donkey ears on everybody in the picture except yourself…

BARBARA: Okay.

THOM: Now, how do you feel about the experience right now?

BARBARA: Laughter. What I did is I went back to the beginning and said, "Okay, this didn't happen."

THOM: Aha! So, you're laughing now. A few minutes ago I'm guessing you weren't laughing about this experience.

BARBARA: No, I wasn't.

THOM: Okay, number one, you're laughing now, and, number two, what you just told me is that story about the experience has changed. Has it?…The story that you tell yourself about what happened there?

BARBARA: Yeah.

THOM: Typically, what happens is stories change from *Oh, gee, I was a victim* to *Oh, that happened but I learned from it.* That kind of a transition, was it something like that?

BARBARA: No, it was, Okay, that happened; let's just accept it and deal with it, that's it, instead of being so anxious about it.

THOM: Okay, so you have transformed a memory by simply shifting the filing system that your brain uses for it.

BARBARA: Okay, thank you, Thom.

THOM: You're welcome.…Thanks, Barbara, for calling.

The point is to change how the experience is filed. As your listener changes the submodalities, he is actually moving the memory to different physical parts of the brain. You can see that happen on an electroencephalogram (EEG): different parts of the brain have different resources; they have different ways of dealing with things.

In the field of psychotherapy, if you want to heal a negative memory, you can let the brain do that work by moving the memory around. (I describe this technique in my book *Walking Your Blues Away: How to Heal the Mind and Create Emotional Well-being* [Park Street Press, 2006].) Somewhere along the line, that memory will pass through a part of the brain where there is a resource—some skill or experience—that will be able to change the memory. You'll know when you've succeeded in truly changing the emotional charge and filing system associated with a memory because the story about the meaning of that memory changes.

In the political field, the key is knowing how we use submodalities to encode data in the mind. They're the "sharp edge" of the scalpel of modalities; and if we include them carefully, our message will have more impact.

For example, Reagan's speechwriter quoted John Winthrop's 1630 sermon "A Model of Christian Charity." It was a powerful metaphor, first used by John F. Kennedy, in a January 9, 1961, speech, in which JFK said:

> I have been guided by the standard John Winthrop set before his shipmates on the flagship *Arbella* three hundred and thirty-one years ago, as they, too, faced the task of building a new government on a perilous frontier.
>
> "We must always consider," he said, "that we shall be as a city upon a hill—the eyes of all people are upon us."
>
> Today the eyes of all people are truly upon us—and our governments, in every branch, at every level, national, state and local, must be as a city upon a hill—constructed and inhabited by men aware of their great trust and their great responsibilities.

But Reagan's speechwriter added a critical submodality to it—*shining*. This so dramatically increased the impact of the image of the city on a hill that most Americans don't remember that

Reagan's speech had essentially plagiarized Kennedy's or that Kennedy had been quoting Winthrop. We think Reagan invented the concept and that the concept itself was world changing. All because the submodality of *shining* was added into the visual metaphor of a city on a hill.

Here's the key: if you can change the submodality under which an experience or idea is filed, you can change not only *where* the experience or idea is filed but also *how* someone experiences or thinks about it. That's called *anchoring*, and it's a very powerful communication tool that we take up in chapter 5.

ECOLOGY CHECK

The ability to use modalities and submodalities to modify feelings is one of the most powerful tools of competent communicators. It's the main reason why television is so powerful—because it can quickly incorporate visual and auditory information in a way that rapidly evokes emotion.

Consider the video of the planes striking the towers on 9/11—how it was replayed over and over again, creating a powerful visual and auditory image connected with a welter of visceral primitive emotions. Politicians played on these emotions like the string section of a symphony whenever they wanted to promote a particular program, from their war in Iraq to destroying the civil liberties that people have fought and died for since King John first signed the Magna Carta at Runnymede in 1215.

This considerable power was once constrained by a liberal law requiring that "news" actually be news of relevance to people's lives and to the interests of the nation. Reagan, a conservative who believed that a government of laws was morally and functionally inferior to corporations' responding to a "morally neutral free market," stopped enforcing the Fairness Doctrine in 1986, removing the requirement that radio and television stations program "in the public interest" in exchange for their use of the radio frequency spectrum (the airwaves that we all collectively own as part of the commons). Bill Clinton further sold off these commons with the Telecommunications Act of 1996.

The result has been that so-called "news" operations no longer provide news; instead we now receive infotainment packaged as news. Instead of having the purpose of informing the public about issues critical to our lives (the goal of news), we now have corporations feeding us infotainment packaged to draw as many eyeballs as possible, thus increasing ratings and advertising revenue. The bottom line is now corporate profit instead of the well-informed citizenry our Founders envisioned when they named the "Press" as the only industry to be protected in the Constitution, subsidized news through special fourth-class postal rates, and subsidized the production of newsprint.

Not only is this new form of infotainment highly unecological, it also opens the door to a *1984*-like control of citizens and government through massive corporate disinformation campaigns. Jeff Cohen and Norman Solomon wrote a book, *Wizards of Media Oz: Behind the Curtain of Mainstream News,* which details how a number of large corporations have used their "news" operations to advance a variety of corporate interests at the expense of the public interest—all since Reagan's fateful decision rooted in the conservative notion that morality-neutral corporations would run things better than governments responsive to morally evil human voters.

Fast-moving images, *whoosh* sound effects marking changes from story to story, and other subtle visual and auditory tools—all help create an emotion of urgency and importance for what is increasingly banal and insignificant.

CHAPTER 5

HOW FEELINGS
ARE ANCHORED

Put the argument into a concrete shape, into an image, some hard phrase, round and solid as a ball, which they can see and handle and carry home with them, and the cause is half won.

— RALPH WALDO EMERSON

If you want to know how some politicians gained so much power through the 1990s, you can start with my former congressman, Newt Gingrich. Gingrich studied the way language and the brain work, cracked the communication code, and then set out to teach that code to his fellow Republicans.

Here's the key message from his 1996 memo (and later video) with the Orwellian title, "Language: A Key Mechanism of Control."[1]

> Often we search hard for words to define our opponents. Sometimes we are hesitant to use contrast. Remember that creating a difference helps you. These are powerful words that can create a clear and easily understood contrast. Apply these to the opponent, their record, proposals and their party.

The words that follow in Gingrich's essay are designed to trigger the submodality filing system in our brains. They are all words heavy with emotion. The first set contains words Gingrich urged Republicans to use against their Democratic opponents:

> *decay, failure (fail), collapse(ing) deeper, crisis, urgent(cy), destructive, destroy, sick, pathetic, lie, liberal, they/them, unionized*

bureaucracy, "compassion" is not enough, betray, consequences, limit(s), shallow, traitors, sensationalists, endanger, coercion, hypocrisy, radical, threaten, devour, waste, corruption, incompetent, permissive attitude, destructive, impose, self-serving, greed, ideological, insecure, anti-issue, anti-flag, anti-family, anti-child, anti-jobs, pessimistic, excuses, intolerant, stagnation, welfare, corrupt, selfish, insensitive, status quo, mandate(s) taxes, spend(ing), shame, disgrace, punish (poor...), bizarre, cynicism, cheat, steal, abuse of power, machine, bosses, obsolete, criminal rights, red tape, and patronage.

These are all words that bring up pictures that evoke negative feelings. When Republicans successfully associated these negative emotions with their political opponents, people filed their mental pictures and stories of the opponent under that negative emotion. Afterward, every time the opponent's name came up, or a picture or sound including that person was presented, the feeling that that evoked was negative. Gingrich changed *how* voters *filed* that person, and by doing so he changed how they *felt* about that person.

The technique of associating a person or an issue with an emotion through the use of sensory modalities or submodalities is what communicators call *anchoring*.

The same anchoring technique can be used in a positive way to encourage people to adopt a point of view. Here's what Gingrich says about what he calls "governing" words:

Use the list below to help define your campaign and your vision of public service. These words can help give extra power to your message. In addition, these words help develop the positive side of the contrast you should create with your opponent.

Here's Gingrich's list of words he wanted Republicans to use to describe themselves and their positions:

share, change, opportunity, legacy, challenge, control, truth, moral, courage, reform, prosperity, crusade, movement, children, family, debate, compete, actively, we, us, our, candidly, humane, pristine, provide, liberty, commitment, principle, unique, duty, precious, promise, caring, tough, listen, learn, help, lead, vision, success, empowerment, citizen, activist, mobilize, conflict, light, dream, freedom, peace, rights, pioneer, pride, building, preserve, pro-flag, pro-child, pro-environment, pro-reform, pro-workfare, eliminate good time in prison, strength, choice, choose, fair, protect, confident, incentive, hard work, initiative, common sense and *passionate.*

These are words designed to help Republicans tell the conservative story. Most of the words would work for Democrats too, though not all (liberals rarely want to go on crusades). The point is that each of these words can be used as an anchor—it is rich with emotion and hits the limbic brain—and many of them drop encoding information through the modality filter all the way to submodalities.

ANCHORING CODE TO WIN ELECTIONS

Republican strategists understand the power of anchoring. So do unconsciously competent communicators like Ronald Reagan.

In the election of 1980, Reagan opposed welfare and wanted to anchor it in the negative emotion that he already held for it. He achieved that end through the story of the "Chicago Welfare Queen" with her dozen Social Security numbers, eighty names, and thirty addresses, who picked up her welfare checks (totaling, Reagan often said in his 1980 stump speeches, more than $150,000 a year) in a Cadillac. The Cadillac was the anchor for that tremendously powerful story—it was a strong visual that inspired anger, an anger that then carried over to the issue of welfare.

Even though newspapers across America tried to find a single example of the story's truthfulness and were unsuccessful—Reagan had hallucinated the entire thing out of a newspaper story about a woman who was convicted of using two aliases to bilk the government out of $8,000 and didn't have a Cadillac—the story took on an iconic status and paved the way for Bill Clinton's deconstruction of Lyndon Johnson's Great Society, which had cut poverty in America in half in just its first four years. Even though today's statistics show a post-Clinton rise in infant mortality among America's poor, Reagan's story is still so powerful that politicians are afraid to speak words in support of "welfare."

Similarly, to sell the "War on Drugs," then President George H. W. Bush held up a bag of crack cocaine on TV on September 5, 1989, saying it had been taken from a drug dealer working out of Lafayette Park, a 7-acre public park right across Pennsylvania Avenue from the White House. Again, a strong visual, the bag of crack cocaine, was anchored to a threat—the threat of drugs so ubiquitous they could even be found in a public park across the street from the White House.

In fact, there were no drug dealers in Lafayette Park. Bush's handlers had successfully urged Drug Enforcement Administration (DEA) agents to use huge incentives to talk a teenage drug dealer from the east side of the city to come all the way downtown to meet them in the park so Bush could have his photo op. The story's being a lie didn't much harm Bush—he still got laws that would throw more young Black men (and fewer White ones, as Whites were more likely to use powder than crack cocaine) into jail and, in many states like Florida, off the voter rolls.

Anchoring can be used in more-subtle ways than it is in these stories. To get a sense of how anchoring can be used subliminally, we need look no further than the Republican ads in the 2004 presidential campaigns.

One of the most effective anchors in George W. Bush's 2004 presidential campaign was subtle but consistent, and it worked. At the end of each ad for his campaign, we heard, "I'm George W. Bush, and I approve this message." In many of those ads, especially toward the end of the campaign, the image shown was Bush on the phone, holding a sheaf of papers, head down. He looked busy. He looked like a man so hard at work that he didn't even have time to say, "I approve this message." In fact, the audio on that tagline was blurred, as if the PR people hadn't been able to get face-time with the president to even record those few words.

By contrast, John Kerry in the Bush 2004 ads always was pictured dressed in a business suit. He looked good—but he looked like someone on the campaign trail. Taken by itself, that image could have had any emotion attached, even a positive one. But after being contrasted again and again with the visual of Bush at work, the image of Kerry on the campaign trail began to acquire a negative emotion: he's not busy; he's not working. It tied in with the Bush campaign's message that Kerry was a flip-flopper, which also suggested flip-flops and windsurfing...and laziness.

Anti-Kerry ads implying that Kerry was lazy, a dilettante, and a flip-flopper also used similar visuals to depict Kerry as did Kerry's own ads, causing a blurring between the two anchors.

See enough Bush ads, and every time people saw John Kerry looking happy and carefree in a business suit, they'd see an image of George W. Bush slaving away in his office or feel the emotion from the anti-Kerry ads. After a while people would start seeing Kerry in a business suit and feel a negative emotion and think, *what a lazy flip-flopper.* It was brilliant because Kerry, of course, thought he was busy looking presidential when he wore those suits. The more often Kerry put on a jacket and a tie, the more often folks who'd seen the Bush ads saw Kerry as being a lazy flip-flopper. That's the impact of anchoring.

FINDING THE RIGHT WORDS

In addition to his flawed ad campaign, John Kerry himself often used long sentences and polysyllabic words to describe his ideas. That would work if his words were being heard only by the rational part of the brain, but they were not. So all of Kerry's really smart ideas just flew by listeners who did not already have some sort of filing system set up to receive those ideas. They resonated with the already convinced but weren't so emotionally persuasive for the fence-sitters.

Hillary Clinton is another politician who struggles with communication. In a speech she made as senator in 2006, Hillary tried to make the point that even though we are threatened by terrorists, we must remember to hold on to our values. At that time the Senate was in an uproar after having discovered that the Federal Bureau of Investigation (FBI) had gone way beyond the Patriot Act and had wiretapped thousands of Americans without any authorization at all. This was a moment liberals could have seized to engage the country.

At a key point in this important speech about wiretapping, Hillary said:

> So therefore we do need legal protections that are up-to-date with the technological and national security needs of our time— for a world in which we can be confident that our security and our privacy are both protected. And that is what I would like to propose today.[2]

Nothing in that speech anchors her listeners to any strong feeling. There are a lot of abstractions and very few modal words. The one arguable anchor Hillary uses, *security,* belongs to the con-servatives—it conjures an image of 9/11 and a feeling of fear that is part of the conservatives' basic storyline.

Hillary would have given a much more effective speech had she told the liberal story, using visual, auditory, and kinesthetic elements that would make it more memorable. For example, she could have said:

> The world is changing before our very eyes. The Internet gives us the freedom to talk with friends and family in the far cor-ners of the world. Cheap airfare lets us fly to see them. As the world comes together, the world's bullies think they can push

us around. Corporations invade our privacy. Terrorists make us feel insecure. But we Americans have always treasured the freedom to speak our minds when, where, and how we please. Our Founders wrote that freedom into the Constitution. Even as the world changes, our values must stay true to what generations of Americans have fought for, from the founding of this nation to today. That's why we all should work hard to defeat the ongoing Republican assault on our legal right to say what we want, how we want, to whomever we want.

This speech would have hit all three primary modalities right away: "talk"—auditory, "see"—visual, and "push"—kinesthetic. It would anchor Clinton's talk in *freedom,* a word with very positive associations for both liberals and conservatives, and *values.* Also, the idea of "coming together" is another positive anchor and an important part of the liberal story. And it ends with a call to action that also anchors *Republican to assault.*

Anchoring an Issue: Health Care

When it comes to communicating, feeling comes first. Most people are not won over by rational arguments but rather by the stories we tell. To communicate effectively, tell people a story that evokes an emotion and is highly visual.

Consider health care. While conservatives are busy telling the American public that a national health-care system would "ration" care (a negative anchor word that could easily be on Gingrich's list), liberals are busy talking statistics. For example, the United States ranks twenty-fifth in the world in life expectancy, infant mortality, and immunization rates. That kind of statistic is compelling—for a person who already believes that our health-care system has a problem. But persuading people who believe that, despite all its flaws, our health-care system is the best in the world requires a different approach. People need a story.

This is the true story of a man named Dave Flowers that you can find—along with his picture—on www.americansforhealth care.org:

> I own a pizzeria in Peoria called Mickie's Pizzeria, where I have 25 employees. However, I am unable provide health insurance to my employees because I can't afford to pay the premiums.
>
> I haven't just seen the health-care crisis, I've lived it. In 2002 I acquired a viral infection that almost collapsed my heart. I lost a job because I was unable to work full-time.
>
> I couldn't afford the COBRA rates because they were $1,000 a month for my family. It was frustrating and scary. I found a way to get them insurance but I couldn't afford it for myself. No insurance company will insure me as an individual because of my pre-existing condition.
>
> The health of my wife and two daughters is what I value most. Nothing in life is more important.
>
> But I don't want this to happen to my employees or their families. Quality, affordable health care is a right, and I am going to do everything I can to get coverage for all my employees. No one should have to make the choice that I did.

Dave's story is so persuasive in part because in his first two paragraphs he uses sensory modalities to bring us into his world. He "hasn't just seen" the health-care crisis (visual), he's "lived it" (kinesthetic). His health-care issues were "frustrating and scary." These are emotional words that trigger our own feelings.

What makes Dave's story even more powerful is that these sensory and emotional triggers are tied directly to the values embodied in the liberal story. Dave was compassionate because he wanted to insure his family. He cares about his employees and their families. He believes that health care is a right. The story anchors the health-care issue directly in liberal values by using emotional and sensory triggers.

Dave's story moves from his specific case to the biggest story, the story all liberals have to tell: that health care is a right, not a privilege, because it has to do with the founding idea of our nation, that the purpose of government is to backstop us all, to provide a base from which we can reach our highest potential, a net to catch us when we fall, and ultimately to provide the basis for "Life [as in staying alive with health care!], Liberty and the pursuit of Happiness."

Our society used to have a shared understanding that health care was uniquely different from other products and services. Through most of the twentieth century, most states required hospitals and health insurance companies to be nonprofit organizations. That's because we all believed that the main goal of health-care providers was to provide health care.

That all began to change during the Reagan area, when conservatives pushed states to drop the requirement that health-care and health insurance companies be not-for-profit. The primary goal of health-care providers became making a profit for their shareholders, which conservatives believed would produce greater efficiency and lower health-care costs for everybody. It made several billion dollars in profits for Bill Frist's family, but meanwhile the "life" part of "life, liberty, and the pursuit of happiness" dropped out of the American social consensus.

Health care is a right, not a privilege, in every industrialized nation in the world except the United States. Liberals the world over believe that people should have the right to be able to see a doctor and go to a hospital and get well without breaking the bank. We're all in this together, and if any of our people are sick, we should heal them, as that radical liberal Jesus said.

An anchor like the story of Dave Flowers helps people see, hear, and feel that health care is a right, not a privilege. Dave Flowers's true story is one example of a way to use anchoring that's ecologically consistent.

CHAPTER 6

THE "NEGATIVE" CODE

If you don't like the way the world is, you change it. You have
an obligation to change it. You just do it one step at a time.

— MARIAN WRIGHT EDELMAN

During a nightclub act, Michael Richards, the actor who played
Kramer on the TV show *Seinfeld,* called a person heckling him
the N-word.[1] In apologizing the next day, Richards went on the air
and defended himself by saying, "I am not a racist."[2]

No one believed him any more than they believed Richard
Nixon when he said that he was "not a crook." First, because what
Richards said had been captured on video and was played end-
lessly on the Web and in the news, for most of us it sure looked and
sounded (and felt) like at least some part of him was racist (as is
true of virtually every human on the planet). In the public's mind,
Richards's denial failed the ecology check.

As we have seen, however, people can get away with lying in
the short run—as Bush did about Iraq's weapons of mass destruction—if they are competent communicators (or have the complic-
ity of competent communicators in their party and the corporate
media). As the old saying often attributed to Abraham Lincoln
goes: "You can fool some of the people all of the time and all of
the people some of the time, but you can't fool all of the people all
of the time."

The Wrong Message Code

The ecology check of "truth" isn't always enough. Messages should be true, but they also must be presented effectively. Remember Goosalini, the psycho goose who began this book? His message to me (*stay off the deck!*) was immediately effective, but he didn't communicate it in a way that persuaded me over the long term.

What went wrong with Richards's self-defense? "I'm not a racist" is simple language—for the conscious brain. But the unconscious parts of our mind hear that sentence as "I *am* a racist." Richards's apology only confirmed what everyone already thought about him.

The unconscious mind cannot generally translate or decode multiple-layer-language information in the same way the conscious mind can. Modern cognitive scientists like Sean C. Draine, PhD, have done research that demonstrates that the unconscious mind cannot process negatives.[3] Draine's work shows that if you subliminally present a person with a word preceded by *not,* as in *not clean* or *not dirty,* the person won't first process the *not*—he or she will first hear "clean" or "dirty."

The same is true if you are able to subliminally present words preceded by prefixes such as *un* or *dis,* such as *unhurt* and *disloyal.* People reacting to such words at an unconscious level hear "hurt" or "loyal."

Here's an example of one progressive organization that may be sending out the wrong message. Public Citizen, a nonprofit organization founded by Ralph Nader and dedicated to representing consumer interests, walks the walk. If only it knew how to talk the talk.

Here's what Public Citizen wrote in "Health Research Group Publication #1778,"[4] a publication that could use a friendlier title if Public Citizen really wants anyone in the public to read it:

> The main argument in favor of a single payer system is that
> such a system is the only way we can realistically afford to end

the dangerous, embarrassing, and worsening situation wherein about 45 million people in this country lack health insurance and millions more are seriously uninsured.

This is their main argument in *favor* of a single-payer national health-care system.

The good folks at Public Citizen know what they *don't* want. They *don't* want a health-care system that is "dangerous, embarrassing, and worsening." But if you are like most people, all you felt were "dangerous, embarrassing, worsening"—and then unconsciously linked those horrific words to "single payer system"! (Maybe you also saw/heard/felt "lack" and "uninsured.")

Consciously, we understand that Public Citizen believes that a single-payer program will be better for us. Our unconscious mind, however, hears only "dangerous," "embarrassing," "worsening," "lack," and "uninsured," and that's where the meaning-creating feelings are first instilled. That's where the most powerful filing system first goes to work. That's where the most lasting emotions and thus memories are stored.

Consider instead a simple, visual story: "Single-payer health care means that whenever you are sick you can walk into your doctor's office or any hospital and have all the care you need, for as long as you need it, with the calm assurance that all the bills will be paid by the government."

NOT A TRAITOR?

Parents who have tried desperately to get their kids to do something often discover the unconscious mind's inability to process the negative. Instead of saying, "get dressed," parents will say, "okay, whatever, don't get dressed." Consciously, the child hears the parent giving her control over the situation, a choice about what to do. When people who aren't parents hear parents say this sort of thing, they sometimes wonder what the heck the parents are doing.

What parents have figured out—usually without understanding what is happening in their child's brain—is that, for the
unconscious mind, a negative message is the same as a positive
message. When a child hears "don't get dressed" their unconscious
mind processes this as "get dressed." Because children tend to be
very open to unconscious suggestion when their parents talk to
them, this technique can be very effective.

Partisans frequently make use of this technique as a tool for
political persuasion. For example, in their attacks political front
men for the pro–Iraq occupation faction often say things to the
effect of, "I don't think the good senator from Massachusetts ever
actually said that he was a traitor, and I certainly would never call
him a traitor, even if it sounded that way." What listeners hear,
however, is that the senator from Massachusetts is a "traitor."

Here's an example of how this works. In early 2007, the media
unearthed evidence that State Senator Darrell Jackson of South
Carolina—an African American—had endorsed Hillary Clinton
for president in 2008 very soon after her campaign hired his media
consulting firm for $10,000 a month. Of all the scandals of that
election, this possible money-for-endorsement scandal was just
a tiny blip. It's worth mentioning only because of the way it was
spun by the conservatives. A headline on a right-wing "news" Web
site read: "Hillary Clinton: 'We're Not Buying Black Votes'"[5]

Let's unpack that. Hillary Clinton never said, "We're not buying Black votes." What she said was that Senator Jackson was an
old family friend and that her husband had used him before as
a consultant. Nothing in the original story from the Associated
Press said anything about Black votes, though it did mention that
Darrell Jackson was an influential Black politician.

It's an old conservative game to use race as a wedge. For example, Darrell Jackson is a prominent Black politician who represents
a majority African-American district. Media stories tried to make
it seem plausible that Hillary Clinton was buying his endorsement,
which meant the votes of the people he represents—mainly Black

people. The conservative Web site could have written, "Hillary Clinton seeks to buy Black votes," but that would be factually incorrect. Instead, they implied something that never happened but which triggered strong anchors for southern Whites.

The headline avoids the charges of racism and of partisanship yet still gets the idea of buying Black votes across—all by using the negative. "We're Not Buying Black Votes." That sounds nonpartisan. For a lot of White people, it doesn't feel racist (though it is). It looks as if it is just a quote from Hillary Clinton even though it's not. But if you have cracked the code, you know that what readers will actually see is, "Hillary Clinton: 'We're Buying Black Votes.'"

THE POWER OF YOU

Another powerful way to embed ideas or information into the unconscious is to tap the power of the word *you*. The unconscious mind doesn't have a filter for the word *you*. Instead it *always* hears the word *you* as being directed at the self. When I say "you," you unconsciously feel that you as a personal individual are being addressed, even when the word is wrapped in an alternative or third-person context.

For example, Louise and I had hired a contractor for some work on our home, and we were having some problems with him. At dinner at a local restaurant, Louise was telling me about her conversation with this guy. She said to me, "So I said to him [and then she points her finger at *me* for emphasis], 'You better start showing up on time. I'm really upset.'"

At that moment I felt like, *Holy cow, I'm being lectured at,* and I looked around the restaurant to see how many people thought I'd been a bad husband! Louise has taken some of the same communication training that I have, and she immediately grasped the mistake and restated it: "I mean, I told him that *he* has to start showing up on time!"

You can be incredibly powerful: even when we know that the word isn't directed at us specifically, we will always, at an unconscious "feeling" level, take it personally.

Anyone who has a teenager knows how powerful the word *you* is and how easily it can backfire: "you messed up your room," "you were late." These are statements of fact, but that's not how teenagers take them. People are generally much quicker to take offence if a criticism is put in the second person (*you*) than in the third person because the criticism goes right to the unconscious mind and evokes a primary emotional response before the intellectual response has a chance to kick in.

THE INDIRECT YOU

On my radio program, I like to have political discussions with people who disagree with me. It's fun talking politics with people who already agree with me, but that isn't going to get more votes for a better economy or a smarter foreign policy. It's especially important, when talking to someone whose politics are very different, to avoid using the direct "you" unless it's done it with very specific intent. In those situations, using "you" is confrontational, and people will reject everything said if they feel that they're coming under personal attack (which is what "you" in an adversarial context will always do).

Here's an example. Carol, a labor unionist, called my radio show, trying to figure out how she could get management to listen to her. Carol had already figured out that she shouldn't use "you," since she didn't want to antagonize them, but she didn't know what she should do. Carol was telling me that she was consciously incompetent and wanted to know the next step. Here's what she said:

> When I was a union steward dealing with management, either on grievances or in a labor management meeting, if I used the word "you" their defenses would immediately go up, whereas if

I used the third person, like "management does this," they were much more receptive to working with me.

Carol figured out part of the communication code. Using the third person will help avoid negative outcomes. What she also found, however, was that the third person won't get you to the positive outcome you want. She needed a solution. This is how I explained using the "indirect you" to Carol on my radio show:

> Yes, it can screw things up to use "you" directly. But there is a way to use the word *you* as a negotiating tool. Try using "you" in a secondary way like this: "Many of our members tell us that what they would like to say to management is, 'You guys are taking advantage of us and you guys are hurting our families by not giving us good health care.' And I say to our members, when they say that to me, that I'll share that grievance with management, and so I'm here, to share with management their concern."
>
> Now, you personally haven't accused management. You've let your members do it, but you have removed yourself. No one on management can accuse you personally of saying these things to them. You are providing them with information. At the same time, at the unconscious, emotional level, they are going to hear (and feel) "you are not treating us well" but without the automatic conscious reactive defensiveness that comes from a direct, conscious attack on "you."

Here's another example. I often debate conservatives who believe that people should help themselves and that the government shouldn't do anything to help anyone. They even feel that way about homelessness.

So I could say to someone like that,

> I'd like to tell you a story. You know, the other day I was talking to a friend, and he went down to the homeless shelter and he said, "You can't imagine how difficult the lives of these people are. You would have to be, you know, disconnected from life to ignore how difficult it is for them. You'd have to be almost criminally disconnected from humanity to not care about these

people because over a third of them are women and children, usually thrown into poverty by divorce, and a lot of the men are vets who are suffering from posttraumatic stress disorder [PTSD] or other service-connected problems that they can't get help for since Reagan closed the mental hospitals and Bush cut back on veterans' services." And I said to him, "You know, yeah, I agree."

I haven't said to my guest, "How can you personally not care about the plight of the homeless?" I haven't been confrontational. All I've done is talk about someone else who thinks that everyone should care about the homeless and embedded into that emotional statement a bit of data.

Because that third person used the word "you," my guest will unconsciously hear this story as directed right at him. Usually, at that point my guest starts agreeing with me. I have used "you" in this indirect way to create a rapport, and it's also a very human thing to not want to be perceived as uncaring, and that means I am on my way to convincing him—giving him a strong feeling for—the value of my story, my point of view.

Ecology Check

An entire sales-and-marketing industry has been built around teaching people how to use the "indirect you" to make a sale.

Car salespeople are famous for this. A customer is looking at a car, and the salesman is telling her about its features. In the middle of that spiel, he'll casually say, "Some people will come in here and tell me, 'You buy this car, and you have the best car ever made. You really feel great driving this car.'" Then he goes back to talking about the features.

What he's done is embed in the customer's unconscious mind that she would have the best car ever made and would feel great if she bought that car. It works, but it's pretty sleazy.

The "indirect you" is valuable when it is used as a tool to negotiate or mediate differences. It is a way of creating common ground and of getting around conscious defenses to evoke empathy and understanding. The "indirect you" fails the ecology check, however, when it is used to lie to or gain power over someone. It's not honest and it's not ethical. The people who use this part of the communication code most often, along with salespeople, are guys peddling "rapid seduction" techniques. They make a lot of money by teaching men how to seduce women for one-night stands by using techniques like the "indirect you."

A far better use of such tools is to enhance positive communication or avoid accidentally triggering "you/personal" responses when they're not intended.

PART III

THE MEANING OF A COMMUNICATION IS THE RESPONSE YOU GET

CHAPTER 7

THE CODE OF THE
CORE STORY

*The newest computer can merely compound, at speed, the
oldest problem in the relations between human beings,
and in the end the communicator will be confronted with
the old problem, of what to say and how to say it.*

— EDWARD R. MURROW

One reason why we got the Reagan revolution in the eighties
was because Americans—particularly Democrats and liberals—had stopped paying attention to the political responses they
were getting.

As that great liberal president Dwight D. Eisenhower said in
a letter to Edgar Newton Eisenhower on November 8, 1954:

> Should any political party attempt to abolish social security, un-
> employment insurance, and eliminate labor laws and farm pro-
> grams, you would not hear of that party again in our political
> history. There is a tiny splinter group, of course, that believes you
> can do these things. Among them are…[a] few other Texas oil
> millionaires, and an occasional politician or business man from
> other areas. Their number is negligible and they are stupid.[1]

Liberals assumed that Americans still shared Eisenhower's
perspective, but they didn't check those assumptions with the
American public. As it turns out, while liberals were busy during the 1980s, figuring out who should be helped first and what
the highest potential of people could be, the conservatives were

busy telling a different story. In the conservative story, liberals were people who wanted to spend your money. When they weren't spending money, said the conservatives, liberals were busy letting criminals out on the streets (recall that it was a Republican governor who had signed that legislation in Massachusetts).

The conservative story about "evil liberals" became so widespread that by the end of his presidential campaign in 1988, when Michael Dukakis was asked if he was a liberal, he replied, "I am not a label."[2] Besides making the classic communication mistake of using the negative (see chapter 6), Dukakis, at the end of a long fight, was throwing up his hands and giving in to the conservatives' story. For him, like the rest of the American public, *liberal* had just become a label that he wanted to throw away. He had lost control over and ownership of the story that gives liberalism its meaning.

THE MEANING OF A COMMUNICATION IS THE RESPONSE YOU GET

Last week Louise and I were walking along the Greenway, a 44-mile-long pathway that runs along the rivers that bisect Portland. There are no cars on the Greenway, only bicycles and pedestrians. As we were walking along, a guy came up behind us really fast on a racing bike, going so silently that when he said "On your left," it sounded to me like a disembodied voice and I jumped—to my left—and nearly collided with him. As he raced away, I yelled after him, "Get a bell!" in the hopes that he would get one of those little chimes that bicyclists use to let you know they're coming up from behind well before they scare the hell out of you from 5 feet away at 30 miles per hour.

He swiveled his head around, gave me the finger, and angrily yelled that I should perform a sexual act on myself.

At that point I was mystified. My first thought was that he was just an ass, some guy who didn't give a damn that he'd startled a pedestrian and had probably gotten up on the wrong side of the bed that morning. Maybe he was the kind of person who kicks his dog or shoots small animals for fun.

I thought the meaning of my communication was "get a bell," but it was obvious that he didn't think that was the meaning of what I said. But what could it be?

And then it hit me. He was wearing a helmet and an iPod. My voice would have been muffled. He must have thought I yelled, "Go to hell" at him.

Along political lines the same is true. People vote for their member of Congress, for example, but then are mystified when that person votes for something insane like preventing the government from negotiating drug prices or the bill that made it harder for people hit by serious disease to declare bankruptcy.

At this point we should all be collectively slapping our foreheads and saying, "The meaning of a communication is the response you get!" We're getting back from our representatives something different from what we want, in many cases, and so it must mean that our communication isn't getting through to them clearly.

The simple solution is to be more articulate, more outspoken, and more persistent, to join a political party and work for change from within, or to support another candidate.

WHAT'S YOUR STORY?

One way to make sure someone is getting your meaning is to figure out *their* core story and start at that point.

Imagine that two office workers, one liberal and one conservative, are taking a break at the local coffee shop. They are talking about a recent tragedy reported in the news, and one worker says to the other, "I wish we lived in a safer society."

"Yes," says the other, "I agree. I wish the world was a safer place."

That sounds, looks, and feels like a shared moment. But when the first person says she wants to live in a safer world, she is imagining living in a gated community protected by cops with guns, while the second person is imagining a neighborhood where everyone has a good job, health insurance, and security for their old age.

Ideas, stories, even individual words can have a different meaning from person to person, depending on which core story they believe. To a conservative the word *safety* means that powerful social forces are set up to prevent intrinsically evil people from doing bad things. To a liberal the word *safety* means that everyone has had all their basic needs met and does not need to fear the consequences of old age, disease, and an unpredictable economy or environment.

To become a competent communicator, first discover which story your listener shares.

- Does the person believe in the liberal story or the conservative story?

- Does he or she believe that the world is a fundamentally fair and good place (liberal) or that the world is a fundamentally scary and dangerous place (conservative)?

- Does the person believe that his or her task is to help individuals realize their potential (liberal) or that ways must be found to restrain individuals from their own evil impulses (conservative)?

If you don't know, just ask. Most people will simply tell you. When we asked our children what we did that made them feel loved, one said that she felt loved when we told her we loved her, another said that he felt loved when we took him out for breakfast alone, and our third said that she felt loved when we taught her things (she was also the one who insisted on being home-schooled). Everybody is different. Start noticing the responses you

How I Love You

Political communication is easy in one respect: most responses will be based on either the liberal or the conservative story. Knowing which response you are going to get from nonpolitical communication can be more difficult. None of us can ever really know what another person is feeling or experiencing or thinking. We can only make guesses based on our observation of their behavior.

This sounds straightforward, but it's a surprisingly hard concept to grasp. Here's a very personal story, and I tell it with the permission of my wife.

When Louise and I lived in Atlanta, back in the 1980s, we decided to learn more about this idea that "the meaning of a communication is the response you get." So we took a class in NLP and communication. One day the teacher, Leif Roland, turned to me and said, "Thom, how do you know that Louise loves you? What is it that makes you so certain?"

I thought about it for just a half a second. I knew right off the top of my head. I said, "When she touches me, when she walks by and puts her hand on my shoulder, I know I am loved. When she touches or hugs me, I feel loved."

So then he turns to Louise and says, "Now how do you know, Louise, how do you know that Thom loves you?"

I'm sitting there waiting for her to say, "Oh, when he hugs me, when he kisses me, when he says 'I love you'"—something like that.

Instead she said, "When we have coffee and share time together in the morning, reading the paper and talking about things that are important to both of us."

And I'm thinking, *What?!* Back then I didn't even like coffee, and I'd spent decades trying to get out of her morning coffee routine. I am a morning person, and when I wake up I want to get going. I'm a busy guy, and I've always got a list of a million things that I want to get done when I wake up.

So I asked her, "But what about when I hug you, or touch you? What about when I kiss you?"

And she said, "Oh, that's all nice, but I know that you love me when you'll sit and have coffee with me in the morning and share the day and discuss things that are meaningful to both of us."

I had been living with Louise for almost twenty years at that point, and I still didn't understand how we were communicating. I hadn't understood the magnitude of the positive response I was getting from having that morning coffee with her.

So we made a deal. She said, "I'll hug you more often if you'll have coffee and talk with me every morning." And so both of us get to feel loved. And both of us understood, finally, a deeper part of each other's personal communication code.

get to your communications, and you'll have a whole new set of keys to coding your stories and arguments.

Competent communicators in the political world know that key political ideas trigger very different responses among liberals and conservatives. Here are some examples:

VALUES. In the 2004 election between George W. Bush and John Kerry, much was made of polls that showed Americans were voting their "values." No one asked, however, what those values were. If they had, they would have discovered that the conservatives' values centered on what individuals do in the privacy of their own homes and with their own bodies. Conservative "morality" usually has to do with "what other people are doing in private." Conservatives voting on values were voting against gay marriage and for a ban on abortions.

Liberals meant something completely different. Liberals' values center on the welfare of others: are we housing the homeless, feeding the hungry, and caring for the sick. Liberal "morality" usually has to do with "what is happening to all of us in public." People who voted for John Kerry on the basis of their "values" were voting for strong public education, a caring society, a clean environment, and an end to the needless and senseless deaths associated with the Republican wars in the Middle East.

TAXES. No one likes to pay taxes. That said, liberals and conservatives understand the word differently. Conservatives view taxes as a confiscation of wealth: the government is taking *my* money. For liberals taxes are the price of admission to civilized society—it's *our* money. Liberals view taxes as the reasonable and appropriate way to fund an investment in society and the future. From the liberal point of view, if somebody don't want to pay taxes, they're a freeloader.

So when a liberal and a conservative get together at a bar on April 15 and complain about taxes, they are really talking about two different things. The conservative is upset that she is paying the government to do a job she thinks private industry could do better. The liberal is upset that her tax dollars are being used to promote private morality (so-called faith-based programs, prosecutions of doctors providing women with abortions,[3] funding unnecessary wars, and so on) instead of providing for schools, roads, health care, and the public good.

FREEDOM. One of Bush Jr.'s favorite words is *freedom*. In fact, his administration's second official name for the invasion of Iraq was *Operation Iraqi Freedom* (originally, it was to be called *Operation Iraqi Liberation* until some wag in the media pointed out the acronym).

For conservatives *freedom* means that you are safe and protected from other intrinsically evil people, so you can focus on restraining your own natural evil impulses and those of your family through the imposition of discipline. For liberals *freedom* means that you will be able to move easily through the world and interact with others, sharing your deepest goals and beliefs, and that you and members of your family can achieve self-actualization, backstopped with a good education and available health care. Liberals embrace the freedoms enshrined in the Bill of Rights: freedom of speech, assembly, and religion.

GETTING WHAT "WE THE PEOPLE" WANT

The best way to find out which core stories a person holds is to ask. That sounds obvious, but it's actually a very new idea, speaking historically, when it comes to political communication.

The idea that a country's leaders should listen to its people was revolutionary when America was founded. Monarchy was based on the idea of an unchanging system. Kings had a divine right to govern, and that divine right vested, by extension, in the aristocratic class. No matter what was happening in the country, no matter how terrible life was for ordinary people, the king's rule could not be challenged because it was part of the divinely ordained natural order of things.

Early Americans had a lot of firsthand experience with a king who didn't care how his communications were received. No matter how the colonists protested, King George just didn't care enough to listen. Our American ancestors were pretty creative about trying to get his attention. They wrote petitions, made speeches, even dumped tea into a harbor to let the king know that they weren't happy with his policies. It was George's refusal to listen to what his subjects were saying, as much as anything else, that caused the American Revolution.

America's Founders understood that the basis of democratic politics is to create a system in which politicians ask what the people want. They knew that to really have consent of the governed, they would have to ask the governed to speak up every two years or so. That's why America is a constitutionally limited representative democratic republic. We the People elect individuals to represent us. Thus it's our job to tell our representatives what we want, and it's their job to listen to us and represent us. If our elected representatives don't listen to us and don't share our stories about

KING GEORGE

One of the main purposes of the Declaration of Independence was to tell the world that King George had refused to hear, see, or respond to the concerns of his colonists. The Founders wrote:

In every stage of these Oppressions We have Petitioned for Redress in the most humble terms: Our repeated Petitions have been answered only by repeated injury. A Prince, whose character is thus marked by every act which may define a Tyrant, is unfit to be the ruler of a free people.

Nor have We been wanting in attentions to our British brethren. We have warned them from time to time of attempts by their legislature to extend an unwarrantable jurisdiction over us. We have reminded them of the circumstances of our emigration and settlement here. We have appealed to their native justice and magnanimity, and we have conjured them by the ties of our common kindred, to disavow these usurpations, which would inevitably interrupt our connections and correspondence. They too have been deaf to the voice of justice and of consanguinity.

We must, therefore, acquiesce in the necessity, which denounces our Separation, and hold them, as we hold the rest of mankind, Enemies in War, in Peace Friends.

the world, We the People can toss them out and find others who are willing to listen and who do share our worldview.

Senator Bernie Sanders of Vermont, one of the most progressive members of Congress, consistently wins in a state that is mostly conservative and rural. Every week he's in a different town conducting a "tell me" Town Hall meeting, asking for feedback and honestly sharing his own worldview with his constituents. In the Northeast Kingdom region of Vermont—the most rural and Republican and poor part of the state—Bush won handily in 2000 and 2004, and so did Bernie Sanders. Bush won because he lied about his so-called compassionate conservative values; Bernie won because he got to know the people and they got to know him and share his true values.

Senator Sanders sees these town meetings as an important continuation of Jeffersonian democracy. Sanders has said:

> At a time when more and more Americans are giving up on the political process, and when the wealthy and multinational corporations have unprecedented wealth and power, it is imperative that we launch a grassroots revolution to enable ordinary Americans to regain control of their country.[4]

His communication was, "I want to best represent you and therefore I need to know what you want, and I also need your vote." And the response he got was one huge electoral victory after another.

CHAPTER 8

MASTERING THE LEARNING TRANCE

*In a time of universal deceit, telling the truth
becomes a revolutionary act.*

— GEORGE ORWELL

Getting someone's attention is a key element of the communication
tool kit. To communicate you must have a listener. That just seems
like common sense, but it's not as easy to do as we often think.

Most of the time, we're pretty tuned out. We're all busy people,
and few of us have the bandwidth for political decision-making.
Even when we turn on the radio or check out the local news, most
of us are not paying that much attention.

There's science behind that. It turns out that the human brain
can pay attention to only about seven (plus or minus two, depending on the person) things at a time. For example, until you finished
reading this sentence, you probably didn't notice the position your
body is in right now. You probably didn't notice every time you
blinked, looking at the page, but now you are noticing. You may
not have noticed whether you were hungry or not, or if your shoes
are tight or loose, but now you have noticed.

You didn't notice these things before because our brains can
process only a few things at a time, so we automatically *delete,
distort,* or *generalize* most of the information coming in to us, be
it sensory or abstract data. You are noticing all these sensations
now—like how hungry you are or how your shoes feel—because I
am throwing your attention around in different directions.

WHAT IS A LEARNING TRANCE?

Most people think that a "trance" is about being in a state where one is no longer paying attention. It seems like common sense: If somebody is so hypnotized that he can have dental work done without anesthesia, he must not be paying attention. If a hypnotist can put someone in a trance and then put her arm in ice water and the subject doesn't even flinch, she must not be paying attention. Right?

Wrong. In fact, a trance is the result of a surplus of attention.

The key to creating a trance state is to use the fact that we human beings already have a very limited attention span. We then amp up that attention into a very narrow sensory spectrum. If we put a lot of energy into attending to one small sensation, we will not be able to hold on to the other three or eight possible things that were distracting us. The dentist's patient who has been hypnotized doesn't notice the pain from his tooth because he is too busy focusing all his attention elsewhere.

The way stage hypnotists induce a trance is by causing a person to focus just on the hypnotist's voice (for auditory people) or on a particular point (for visual people) or on a particular sensation (for kinesthetic people). In old movies hypnotists would ask people to stare at a watch slowly swinging back and forth on a chain—a technique developed by Scottish psychiatrist Dr. James Braid in the early 1800s to disprove Franz Anton Mesmer's belief that trance states came from the energy of the moon being channeled through the hand of the hypnotist. Especially if the person is primarily visual in orientation, that swinging-chain technique really works.

The key to inducing a trance is to cause a person to focus, focus, focus, more and more intensely. Some people are very easily hypnotized; for others it's more difficult. People who are most easily hypnotized are generally those who can most easily and naturally focus their attention.

Sometimes the trance is called daydreaming, where we're very focused on something that is happening or that we want to happen in our lives. Sometimes we go into a reading trance. That's when you're reading a book and you're not noticing the clock ticking in the room or much of anything else—you're totally wrapped up in the world of the book. Sometimes we go into a trance listening to a talk show or attending to the media or listening to a teacher; that's a learning trance and the subject of this chapter.

The trance that virtually everybody has experienced is the movie trance, where we're so focused on the movie that it actually becomes our primary reality. To do this movies alternate close-up and distant shots (visual submodalities), vary music and sound (auditory submodalities), and evoke increasingly more powerful feelings (called "building tension," it actually does, physically, build tension in the body).

All effective communication requires that the recipient focus on the data contained within the communication itself. By definition, that's a trance. In a *learning trance,* the person's awareness is totally focused on the message you are communicating.

How to Induce a Learning Trance

We all hope that our communication is effective enough that our listeners and readers will be literally "entranced" by what we say. For some people that ability comes naturally. We've all met people who somehow seem to just know how to get others to listen attentively to them. Bill Clinton is that kind of natural communicator, and so was Ronald Reagan.

Most of us are not unconsciously competent communicators. We have to learn how to get people to pay attention to us. In part that means learning how to induce a learning trance.

A learning trance is a pretty light trance—people can break out of it themselves and are fairly aware of what they are doing.

An effective learning trance is a lot like a movie trance. A good movie tells an interesting story. In chapter 2 I talked about the value of stories in political persuasion. Stories are multimodal and are full of anchors. A good story creates pictures and sounds in our minds and attaches a particular emotion to those pictures and sounds. A good movie story will use anchors to make us feel a variety of emotions.

The story creates a bridge between our feelings and the story line. That bridge functions positively to keep our feelings narrowly attuned to what is in the story; it also functions negatively by preventing our brains from wandering to some other feeling. That's one reason why people like to go to the movies or read a good novel when they're feeling bored—they know the movie will draw their focus to a different emotion.

Second, a good story shifts back and forth between modalities as a way to keep our attention focused on the action. Because we can pay attention to only a few things at a time, shifting modalities very quickly is hard for us to do and makes us focus very intently so we can catch what is happening. This modality shifting is even more powerful if the modalities are connected to anchors.

Third, a good story will also pay attention to rhythm, tempo, and pacing. Creating and maintaining a person's focus requires creating the right tempo. A good story will use rhythm, tempo, and pacing to draw the attention back into the story.

Film editors use a variety of means to create these effects. They use music to create a rhythm and a tempo. They intercut, cut in on, and cut away from a scene to change the film's tempo and pacing. Think of any scene from a Hitchcock movie—how we first may see only an eye, or a knife, and then the window looking out across the street, and then cut back to the victim, and so forth. That cutting is hard to follow, so we focus all our attention on it, and that intense focus puts us in the movie trance. The same is true of listening to a good storyteller or reading a good novel.

We most often find anchoring (the "scary" music is anchored to the "scary" moments, for example, or the thunderstorm begins when the drama is being amped up), modality shifting (we see a face, then the screen goes black and we hear a scream), and pacing used to create a movie trance in action movies, thrillers, and—no surprise—commercials. It's the surest way to get and hold someone's attention.

MODALITY SHIFTING

We already discussed anchoring at length in chapter 5. The second way to create a learning trance is to shift a person from one sensory modality to another very quickly. In part II we went over the different sensory states: what we see, what we hear, and what we feel.

I stressed at the beginning of this book that one way to communicate effectively is to identify the primary mode a person uses and speak to the person in that mode. For example, if you're talking to someone who is highly visual, use a lot of visual metaphors and ask, "Do you see that?" For somebody who is highly auditory, use auditory metaphors: "Do you hear what I'm saying?" For someone who is very kinesthetic, use kinesthetic metaphors: "Hey, do you get that concept? Is that a solid one for you?"

Using someone's primary modality is a good way to initiate a conversation; but a learning trance is actually created by switching modalities in a serial fashion. Doing so focuses people's attention and puts them into a kind of heightened trance state.

One of the strongest ads from the 2004 campaign, "Yakuza," was put together by the Bush team; you can find it at http://pcl .stanford.edu/campaigns/campaign2004/archive.html, a Web site created by some folks at Stanford University to analyze all the media ads from past political campaigns.

The ad shifts modalities from sentence to sentence, frame to frame. It starts with a book cover—a visual image—that's accompanied by a question mark, which asks you to listen to the narrator, moving us from visual to auditory. *Announcer:* "John Kerry says he's 'author of a strategy to win the War on Terror.'" The next image is very visual, a page from a Japanese comic book, forcing us to focus on visual input and all but ignore the narrator. *Announcer:* "...against the Japanese yakuza."

Then we go to an image of John Kerry against a black background with a blurry photo of a terrorist in the background covered by a question mark again, which is now becoming a kind of trigger for a return to the auditory. *Announcer:* "...never mentions al-Qaeda. Says nothing about Osama Bin Laden. Calls Yasser Arafat a 'statesman.'" The ad continues like that, pushing us back and forth between auditory and visual.

As these images fly by, the announcer turns to purely visual words: "The *New Republic* says Kerry's plan 'misses the mark.' And Kerry's focus? Global crime, not terrorism."

Auditory, visual, auditory, visual. The effect is to anchor a sense of confusion. That's how they end the ad, suggesting that Kerry is just as confused as we are: *Announcer:* "How can John Kerry win a war if he doesn't know the enemy?"

Notice that these last words also take advantage of the unconscious mind's inability to process the negative and the fact that the word "know," in a purely auditory setting, sounds like "no." That last sentence can be very difficult to understand if it goes by quickly because of what to our brain can sound like a double negative—"doesn't know"—and that will leave people with an even simpler conclusion: "*Kerry* is the *enemy* in this *war.*"

This ad put viewers into a learning trance through mixing visual and auditory stimuli. What viewers learned from the ad was that John Kerry was as mixed up as viewers felt after watching the ad. It echoed that campaign's description of John Kerry as a "flip-flopper" and helped enhance the myth Republicans promoted to the media that there was no need to look into widespread election fraud in Ohio because Kerry had lost by being out-campaigned. (This was something the Bush campaign had planned as early as 2002, by the way, as that was when the now-defunct www.democratflipflop.com Web site was registered to the Republican National Committee.)

PACING

The third element to creating a learning trance is pacing. Politicians understand the power of creating a trance to ensure that their listeners get their ideas. Politicians pause a lot. They pause for applause. But they also build in dramatic silences at times when they don't expect applause. That's a component of pacing, and it's of critical importance in creating a learning trance.

Pacing works because it is a technique to focus attention. If you flip people's attention on and off, on and off, on and off, they must concentrate to maintain their attention. That kind of concentration can induce a learning trance. When politicians pause often, it's to get their audience's attention

by causing you to attend

and then not attend

and then attend

and then not attend.

Here's another ad, "World View," created by the Bush team for the 2004 campaign, which does a very effective job of using pacing to tell its story.[1] This ad begins with an image of a blue TV screen with words on it that are impossible to read because they go by so quickly. The ad then cuts to an image of John Kerry sitting in front of a bank of nine TV sets, all with blue screens. The ad continues to intercut between a single screen and the image of Kerry in front of lots of screens. Each time the ad zooms in on a single screen, it's got a message on it that the conservatives really wanted people to see, and the narrator speaks the words at about the same pace that we read them.

Each small message suggests that Kerry is confused about the nature of the terrorist threat.

The constant intercutting between big and small holds our attention. The narrator pauses each time the small screen comes on, then matches his voice to our reading speed. At the same time, the background music is at an even slower rhythm so that a difference in tempo is set up between the very quiet but insistent music and the narrator's voice. The two come together only when the image intercuts—every time a new picture flashes on-screen, there is a louder sound in the music.

With both images, large and small, featuring blue TVs, there is not much to distract us from focusing on the back-and-forth. The "big picture" is "John Kerry." He's the only element it's easy to focus on. The small picture is "what Kerry said." And the words the writers pull out are ones designed to summon the conservatives' worldview, a view that the world is a dangerous and fearsome place. The blue is laying down an anchor—blue, the color of the Democratic Party—associated with the negative emotions evoked by the ad.

The focus on the screens, the intercutting, and the music—the pacing—all prepare us for the difference between what the Republicans are portraying as Kerry's "worldview" and their own. The tagline: "How can Kerry protect us when he doesn't understand the threat?"

BUILDING A LEARNING TRANCE

Putting a person or an audience into a learning trance involves just a few simple steps: Tell a story to capture their attention. Build into the story visual and auditory metaphors and elements, each designed to evoke emotional responses. Embed into the most emotional parts of the stories the information you want remembered. And pace the story so that listeners and viewers move to your beat, thus amplifying the learning trance.

CHAPTER 9

FUTURE PACING

How lovely to think that no one need wait a moment,
we can start now, start slowly changing the world.

— ANNE FRANK

At the start of the One Hundred Tenth Congress, newly elected House Speaker Nancy Pelosi faced a significant communication challenge. The Democrats had won the House by a wide margin in large part because of popular opposition to the ongoing war in Iraq. Pelosi herself represented a San Francisco district adamantly opposed to the war. Yet instead of looking for ways out of war, President Bush had just announced a troop surge. Republican members of Congress were torn between the powerful symbolism of supporting a president during wartime and representing the 60 percent of the American people who opposed the war.

Antiwar protestors from Pelosi's district immediately called on the new Speaker to put forward a resolution defunding the war.[1] Yet it was clear that the Democratic majority in the House was not ready for that step, let alone their Republican colleagues. Without bipartisan support any resolution on the war ran the risk of looking as if it was about partisanship rather than a real effort to change the country's direction. To have a real effect on the president's policies, Pelosi couldn't just communicate the country's dismay over the war; she needed to communicate it in such a way that it would get a sympathetic response from Republicans in Congress and, if possible, from the president himself.

We never fully know in advance what response we'll get from a communication because we can never know what is really going on inside another person or an audience. But the communication code contains a variety of tools that will make it much more likely you'll get the response you want. One of those tools is future pacing. And that's the tool Nancy Pelosi used to move Republican members of Congress away from supporting the president's war.

Future pacing is a tool that allows you to change people's present-time point of view by projecting them into the future and then bringing them back to present time. Particularly useful when someone seems fixed in his current ideas and beliefs, future pacing is a powerful tool to shake that person's decision-making process and move him toward a different set of feelings and beliefs.

The Cigar Code

We'll get back to Nancy Pelosi later in this chapter. But let me tell you a story that is unrelated to politics to show how future pacing works. I usually am pretty careful about when I use this tool, but in this case I used it to change the behavior of someone whom I found frankly offensive.

This was about fifteen years ago. I was doing marketing and brand consulting at the time, mostly for large corporations and government agencies. In that line of work, one travels a lot; I probably spent thirty weeks per year on the road.

This story takes place on the Wednesday before Thanksgiving, the busiest travel day of the year. I was trying to get back home to Atlanta from the West Coast, but I was stuck at the Cincinnati airport because a massive snowstorm was slamming the United States from the Rocky Mountains all the way through the central and eastern Midwest.

Because I flew a lot, I was a member of the Delta Airlines Crown Room Club. Those clubs are very comfortable if you have a long wait—and it looked like my wait was going to be about five hours. I walked into the clubroom and went to the no-smoking area (in those days there were still segregated smoking areas) and looked for a seat. Almost every seat was taken except for a single chair opposite a sofa with a half-dozen other occupied chairs forming a circle around a coffee table. Sitting in the middle of the sofa in the no-smoking section was a big Texas guy—he had the silver belt buckle, the lizard-skin boots under boot-cut blue denim jeans, the whole outfit—smoking a huge and smelly cigar. His cowboy boots were up on the table, and he was puffing away with a studied obliviousness to everyone around him.

The people who were seating near this guy were clearly discomforted by the cigar. There was a sign when you entered the club that said, very clearly, "No pipe or cigar smoking; cigarette smoking only in designated areas." And the designated smoking area was way over on the other side of the club.

I sat down in that empty chair right opposite this guy because it was the only empty chair in the place. I didn't like what he was doing, but I wasn't that bothered by the smoke myself, so I wasn't planning to do anything about it. A few minutes later, though, a woman sitting a couple of chairs away from him started to cough pretty badly. And she said to him, "Sir, your cigar." She added, "I have asthma, and that smoke is really hurting me. Would you please stop, or at least move to the smoking section?"

He looked at her for a long minute as if she were an insect he'd just noticed, took a long puff on his cigar, and blew smoke at her. Then he just looked off in space, being Mr. Cool.

After a minute or two, the woman got up, went over to the counter, and started a conversation with the woman running the Crown Room Club. I couldn't hear what she said, but we all knew what it was. A few minutes later, the employee, who was very busy helping customers who were trying to change their flights and so forth, left her counter and walked over to Mr. Texan, with a pack of Marlboros in her hand.

"Sir," she said, "I've got a pack of cigarettes for you. If you could, please move over to the smoking section. We don't allow cigar smoking, and you can't smoke here in the no-smoking section."

He stared her down for a minute and took another puff of his cigar. He blew it in her direction, and said, slowly and clearly in a voice dripping with disdain, "Call a cop, lady." She stood there, looking rather shocked, and then looked back at the long line of people waiting for her and decided, obviously, that this was not a fight worth having. She turned around, went back to her work, and he resumed being Mr. Smug.

This is a guy who was not going to be easy to persuade. He was not going to be open to listening or seeing or feeling much of anything coming from someone else, no matter what modality I used.

So I leaned across the table, and said to this guy, "I'll bet you know something that I've always wondered about."

I said it in a friendly way. And he looked at me like, *Huh?* So I leaned forward again and said, "I'll bet you know something I've wondered about ever since I was in high school, and that I'd bet most people wonder about, and I bet you know the answer. I bet you could tell me the answer."

He was engaged, so I continued. "In fact," I said, "I'll bet that not only do you know the answer, but pretty much everywhere you go, people know that you know the answer. All they have to do is take one look at you, and they know you know the answer. In the future, whenever and wherever you're walking down the street, I'll bet people will always take a look at you and know that you know the answer."

This is future pacing. I was throwing him into the future, getting him to imagine what the future would be like, in this case, a future in which people were looking at him and knowing he'd know the answer to a question I hadn't yet posed.

He looked at me and he said—so now I'd got him, he was hooked—"Okay, what's the question?"

And I said, "Well, you know, we all learn, in high school, in elementary psychology, everyone knows this, everyone whom you see walking down the street, everyone who sees you in a restaurant, or who comes into this Club…"

I was drawing this thing out, throwing him into the future some more, so that he'd really imagine people thinking about this question and answer everywhere in the future. Then I went in for the kill.

"Everyone," I said, "knows that back in the 1890s, Sigmund Freud said, 'the larger the cigar, the smaller the penis.' So I'm wondering, is that true?"

He took his cigar out of his mouth, this giant dark brown cigar, and he looked at it, and he looked at me. It looked like he was trying to decide whether to punch me or put the cigar out in my face, and I was quickly shedding the pleasant haze of the wine they'd served me on the flight, quickly calculating which way would get me fastest to the door. Then he just stood up, and walked out of the club, his cigar in his hand, only now held close to his body as though he were trying to conceal it. The people sitting in the circle around the coffee table erupted into applause, and the man sitting to my right offered to buy me a beer.

After his performance with the asthmatic woman, I didn't just want to get him to leave the club—I was angry enough at this guy that I wanted to make sure that anytime in the future that he pulled out a cigar, he'd start looking around at all the people wherever he was and imagining that they were all wondering whether or not he had a small penis. My rationalization—and that's frankly all it is, a rationalization for what was really psychological aggression on my part—was that maybe it would encourage him to quit smoking.

In any case, that's future pacing.

BUSH SMOKES CIGARS

A Transcript from the Thom Hartmann Program
January 19, 2007
The caller is Barry in Bellingham, Washington.

BARRY: I really love that anecdote you just told about the cigar-smoking Texan, you know, defying everybody.

THOM: He was like out of central casting. I mean, this guy was so into his...well, don't get me started.

BARRY: Yeah, anyway, as you were talking about this guy, it just flashed on me that [George W.] Bush is like this guy on a large scale.

THOM: How?

BARRY: Here he is, defying the American public who voted in a Democratic-controlled Congress, and defying Congress, you know, in our desire to bring our troops back from Iraq and end this mess over there. You know, just sort of blowing his smoke in everybody's face.

THOM: Without getting too psycho-babbly, maybe what we're seeing here is George's feelings of incompetence and impotence throughout his life being acted out as the big bully war maker.

BARRY: Yeah, I was thinking along those lines. I was thinking maybe somebody should approach him and ask him about the size of his cigar.

How to Modify The Future

When Nancy Pelosi needed to elicit a particular response to the Iraq war, she used future pacing. She began as soon as she was elected Speaker. Here's what she said to the *Washington Post* about the Iraq war:

> House Minority Leader Nancy Pelosi (D-California) said yesterday that Democrats should not seek a unified position on an exit strategy in Iraq, calling the war a matter of individual conscience and saying differing positions within the caucus are a source of strength for the party.[2]

Pelosi started by looking around at the present. In December 2006, when she was named Speaker, the Democrats themselves were divided on where they wanted to go. Pelosi began by acknowledging these differences in the present, and even reframing them as a *strength*.

Soon, however, she started looking down the line from present to future. In an interview with CBS News in response to President Bush's troop surge,

> Pelosi made it clear the issue was the essential backdrop in Washington for the foreseeable future, however much Bush wants to talk about domestic issues. "We have an 800-pound gorilla in the room and it's called Iraq," she said. "That, to me, is the primary issue facing the Congress and the president in terms of some place that we have to work together."[3]

Notice how Pelosi was throwing Congress and the country into the future—no matter what happened down the line, she was saying, Iraq will be the issue. Subtly in this interview, and more forcefully behind the scenes, Pelosi was reminding members of Congress that their constituents would be looking at the situation in Iraq in the elections of 2008.

Whenever Pelosi talked publicly about the war resolution, she always used future tense, portraying a future in which members of Congress had already voted against the president. Here's what she said to Barbara Walters:

> It is, I think, very difficult for the president to sustain a war of this magnitude without the support of the American people and without the support of the Congress of the United States. That's why Congress will vote to oppose the president's escalation, from the standpoint of policy. We will have our disagreement.[4]

Members of Congress care a lot about whether they will be elected again. As the discussion heated up, Pelosi reminded them again that in 2008 the American people would remember how representatives voted: "Friday's vote will signal whether the House has heard the American people: No more blank checks for President Bush on Iraq," said Pelosi.[5]

If Pelosi had stayed only in the future, however, she might not have won in Congress. For future pacing to work, you must not only see yourself in the future, but also be able to see how you are going to get there. You stand at the future and walk backward to the present, noticing all the steps it will take to get from where you are to where you want to go. Pelosi took that walk in a speech to the House as they were debating the resolution she had put forward, moving from the future to the present:

> There is one proposition on which we all agree: our troops have performed excellently in Iraq. They have done everything asked of them. As the resolution states, "Congress and the American people will continue to support and protect the members of the United States Armed Forces who are serving or who have served bravely and honorably in Iraq.
>
> We owe our troops a debt of gratitude, for their patriotism, courage, and service. As a sign of respect for them, particularly those who have lost their lives in the war, and for their families, I request that we observe a moment of silence.

Pelosi here is first describing the war in Iraq as if it is over and the troops are already on their way home. They have been patriotic, they have been courageous, they have served, and they are coming back—that is the future she was trying to persuade her colleagues to embrace. Then she starts to walk backward. How do they get to that moment—which they have just observed—when the war is over and they can thank the troops? They will have to have taken a new course of action.

> We owe our troops a course of action in Iraq that is worthy of their sacrifice. Today we set the state for a New Direction on Iraq by passing a resolution of fewer than 100 words which supports our troops but disapproves of the President's escalation proposal.

Pelosi in this paragraph just stepped backward from the far future to the near future. Troops will be thanked in the far future, she suggests, if the House will pass this bill in the near future. Then she goes back even farther in time:

> One year ago Senate majority Leader Harry Reid and I stood with House and Senate Democrats to propose our agenda for Real Security—to project our power and values to protect the American people.

Democrats already began walking toward that far future over a year ago. In fact, Democrats, as she says below, had already done quite a bit along that path:

> Consistent with our Real Security agenda, Democrats have sent the President four letters, the first last July and most recently in January, urging him to adopt a strategy for success for Iraq containing these elements:
>
> ■ Change of mission
>
> ■ Redeployment of troops
>
> ■ Build political consensus
>
> ■ Diplomacy
>
> ■ Reform reconstruction
>
> ■ Refocus on the War on Terror

With this speech Pelosi moved backward from a time in the future when the troops would come home, to the present challenge, then back to the time in the future when the House would pass the resolution, then back to a time in the past when Democrats had already sent the president four letters outlining this plan.

By moving back and forth along this pathway, Pelosi made it seem inevitable—etching the groove of this course of action over and over in the mind's timeline—and that is one reason why she won with a bipartisan vote of 246 to 182. She had taken the next step along the path to persuading Republicans in Congress to work with her to end the war.

WHAT FUTURE DO WE WANT?

Republican strategists have certainly mastered future pacing. They tell a story about the future that matches their core conservative story: they try to throw us into a frightening world in which we are attacked from all sides by terrorists, our money is taken from us by the government, and our families are broken apart by abortion-loving gay atheists.

It's far more ecological to use future pacing to tell a story about a world that is more peaceful and harmonious, in which we invest in each other and work together toward the future. This was the core future story held by the Founders of this nation. When future pacing is used well, it enhances the core story the communicator believes and it conveys that core story to listeners.

Here's an example of positive future pacing about the economy, taken from a speech John Edwards made to the National Press Club on June 22, 2006. The whole speech is a great example of future pacing, but because it's very long I've taken out parts of it and added comments in brackets to illustrate how Edwards is using the future-pacing tool:

> What kind of America do we want, [kinesthetic] not just to-day, but twenty years from now, and how do we think [visual] we can get there from here? [drawing the line from present to future] The founders of this country created the country we have today because they dreamed large. [taking us back to the past] They knew there were obstacles, but those obstacles didn't mean that they decided a less perfect union would be a good

compromise. We will never get what we don't reach for. [future] So in 2006 [present] and the decades to come, [future] for what should we reach?…

On the America we want to achieve in the next twenty years, [future] I don't think the picture is hard to draw. [visual and kinesthetic] It is an America where we are well on our way to ending poverty. It is an America where every American has health-care coverage—not access to health insurance or other wiggle-word ways we try to describe something less than health coverage for every American. It is an America where businesses and working people thrive in a competitive and fair international marketplace. It is an America where everyone can join the middle class and everyone can build a better future than their parents had. [all of these are in the future, and each evokes a story, a picture, and a feeling]…

You've heard me talk about the Two Americas? [present/past] One for those families who have everything they need, and then one for everybody else. Katrina showed us the Two Americas. Those images [visual past] of men and women at the Superdome stranded without food, water or hope—simply because they didn't have a car or the cash to escape. [kinesthetic] Those images are something we'll never forget. [bringing to the present and projecting into the future]

They've become the face of poverty in America—a symbol of the poor and forgotten families that live in big cities like New Orleans and in small towns and rural America too. [visual present]…

In order to get the country on the path [kinesthetic] to eliminating poverty, we must build [kinesthetic] a "Working Society," [story/auditory] which builds on the lessons of the past to create solutions for the future. [steps from present to future]

At the heart [kinesthetic] of the Working Society is the value [anchor] of work. Work is not only a source of a paycheck but also a source of dignity and independence and self-respect. [kinesthetic/anchors]…

We need to get involved when our neighbors need us. [kinesthetic future]

We need to speak up when we know something's wrong. [auditory future]

And we need to step forward to meet the challenges we all face. [visual future]...

There was a woman—an extraordinary activist—who would end her speeches by saying, "You know, the leaders we have been waiting for are us." [STORY!]

She's exactly right. Poverty is our challenge. It's time for us to lead. [pulling it all together with a call to action, a story summary, an anchor in the present, and projecting into the future]

Notice how Edwards, through the course of this speech, follows the technique of future pacing, moving from the present to the future, going back to the present, and then, standing in the present, visualizing the steps we would need to take to get to that future. What's particularly persuasive about this speech is that it ends with a story. The story is only two sentences—about an activist and her speeches—but it echoes Edwards's point that we don't need to wait any longer to move toward a better future.

The techniques discussed earlier in this book—submodalities, anchoring, embedding, using stories—are effective means of communication. They will get a response. But future pacing is the booster rocket that takes them all into orbit. When paired with proper framing, it is very, very persuasive.

CHAPTER 10

FRAMING

Every word evokes a frame.

— GEORGE LAKOFF

With startling regularity, every month or two someone will call in to my radio program with a very specific story about why they oppose gun control. The story nearly always goes like this:

> A friend of mine was shopping at the supermarket, and when she came back from shopping she found a Black guy (it's always a Black guy) trying to break into her car. As she walked up to her car, he pulled a knife on her. Fortunately, she always carries her gun with her. She pulled her gun out of her purse and he ran away. That's why we need guns.

That's a very powerful story. So every time I hear it, I say, "Wow, that's a powerful story. Tell me more. Who is your friend?" And the caller will say, "Well, actually it didn't happen to my friend; my friend told me the story about someone else that he knows." Turns out, the caller doesn't actually know anyone who pulled a gun on a carjacker in a supermarket parking lot. The story is not a personal story at all. But it has such power, even as a friend-of-a-friend story, because it's a story that gives us a way of understanding an issue.

There are other stories about gun control. In my case, it really is a personal story.

My best friend in high school, Clark Stinson, went off to the army during the Vietnam War. He came home for the Christmas holiday after basic training and told me how much he hated the army and the prospect of going off to a war he didn't believe in. He was feeling really depressed, went to a gun shop, bought a gun, put it in his mouth, and blew the back of his head all over his bedroom wall. If he hadn't been able to get a gun so quickly and easily, he might have been able to get help and still be with us.

Here's another gun control story, synthesized from several articles in the paper over the past few years:

A family in our community just suffered a terrible tragedy. The father was a gun owner who forgot to lock his gun safe. His five-year-old son had a friend over, and they found the open safe. The man's son took out the gun, and the boys decided to play cops and robbers. The gun was loaded, and the boy ended up shooting his little friend.

All of these stories are persuasive. They all have strong visual and kinesthetic elements and appeal directly to our feelings—and, as we discussed in part I, feelings always come first in our decision-making process.

When we probe the stories deeper, the handgun-control story has the advantage of being true.[1] I'm not saying that someone, somewhere didn't pull a gun on a carjacker. I'm sure that has happened, and the National Rifle Association probably issued a hundred press releases about it. But easily available handguns do lead to an increase of suicides and an increase in deaths of innocent bystanders. For example, one in six parents say they know a child who accidentally shot him- or herself with a handgun. Guns kept in the home for self-protection are forty-three times more likely to kill a family member or friend than to kill in self-defense. And suicide is nearly five times more likely to occur in a household with a gun than a household without a gun.[2]

Handgun ownership makes a society more dangerous. A Montreal-based gun control group, for example, uses a statistical comparison between the United States and Canada to bolster the case for increasing gun control in both countries:

Canada has roughly 1 million handguns while the United States has more than 76 million. While there are other factors affecting murder, suicide and unintentional injury rates, a comparison of data in Canada and the United States suggests that access to handguns may play a role. While the murder rate without guns in the U.S. is roughly equivalent (1.8 times) to that of Canada, the murder rate with handguns is 14.5 times the Canadian rate. The costs of firearms death and injury in the two countries have been compared and estimated to be $495 (U.S.) per resident in the United States compared with $195 per resident in Canada.[3]

Truth is always the most powerful form of persuasion, and it offers the most useful and durable (ecological) frame.

FRAMING JOHN MCCAIN

The conservatives had a hard time going into the 2008 election. None of the Republican frontrunners was a dyed-in-the-wool abortion-hating, war-loving, welfare-bashing, corporatocracy supporter—at least not reliably and all at the same time. Unlike the Democrats, who tend to encourage debate among their candidates, the conservatives began, in May 2006—two years before the election—to push potential front-runners toward particular, uniform, conservative views. They wanted to code their communications from the very first moment of the presidential campaign.

One target of this early effort at political persuasion was John McCain. McCain was reliably pro-war and anti-abortion, but he seemed to have some trouble supporting the wealthiest 1 percent of all Americans. Outrageously, McCain had voted to retain the estate tax for estates over $5 million. If someone dies and leaves more than $5 million to heirs, McCain actually thought it was a good idea for their rich children to pay taxes on the money they're getting by accident of birth that exceeded the first 5 million bucks. The conservatives—who care a lot about people who have $5 million at their disposal—were not happy with McCain. So, when McCain was running to retain his Senate seat back in 2006, they created an ad just for the conservative blogosphere designed to get McCain to change his mind. You can see it at www.nodeathtax.org.

The ad is a masterpiece of future pacing, incorporating trance techniques to push McCain into a future in which he will vote against the estate tax. It ties those techniques together with a strong *frame* to code its message.

Here's how the ad goes:

> [picture of John McCain smiling]
>
> "American family business owners and farmers are counting on John McCain…"
>
> > [a white flash, like a camera flashbulb, then a picture of a man holding a boy against a blue sky]
> >
> > "counting on McCain to protect the jobs they create and the legacy they leave their children…"

This is a very friendly opening, designed to establish a rapport with McCain and with McCain supporters. Americans, families, farmers—all "are counting" on McCain. That suggests they will support him, but the emphasis is on what he does in the future.

The flash that comes between pictures is almost unnoticeable. That fast flash is designed to help put McCain supporters into a learning trance. It registers on the unconscious while the conscious is trying to process the words and the images that are more readily visible. The brain has to focus harder to get the visual process going.

> [Flash, then a picture of the *Chicago Sun-Times* against a black background with a quote from McCain circled. The visual submodalities change quickly as the image is shown far away, then brought close. The auditory submodalities shift as the music changes and becomes darker, even dirgelike, too. For some, the visual/auditory connection may suggest a funeral announcement and evoke a powerful kinesthetic feeling/response of dread.]

"counting on John McCain to keep his promise and show the leadership he's known for..."

Now the insistence on the future grows stronger. He's made a promise, and the question is whether he will keep it. The modality changes to kinesthetic.

> [No flash here—the image changes at a slower pace to a dark blurred-out picture on a black background. The picture—which may not be consciously recognized the first time one sees the ad—depicts mourners carrying a casket in the rain, with the logo www.nodeathtax.org in white in front of it.]

"counting on him to cast the deciding vote to end the IRS death tax forever."

Here, finally, is the promise. It's a promise to "end the IRS death tax forever." Go back to Newt Gingrich's anchor words. What words could trigger negative emotions more strongly than "IRS" and "death"? Nothing, perhaps, except "IRS death *tax*." Here those very powerful words are themselves anchored in death both visually—through the black background established in the previous shot and the barely visible funeral picture—and auditorily, through the music. McCain is thrown into the future of his promise. What we've been counting on him to do is end this terrible thing, the IRS death tax.

Notice the many different ways the ad simultaneously is working to create a trance. Aside from the intermittent flashes, the ad shifts submodalities from auditory to visual to kinesthetic. The effect is that by the time this final, dramatic picture shows up, the viewer must focus very hard to figure out what is happening on-screen. By now most viewers will be deeply in a learning trance.

Notice also that this image gets the viewer to key in particularly on the words *death tax* in the URL www.nodeathtax.org. As we know, at the unconscious/emotional level the viewer won't pick up the negative *no* and will unconsciously only read death tax and shudder.

[The ad flashes again, a flash that is longer and brighter.
The picture then goes back to the exact same image the
ad began with—an image of John McCain smiling.]

"Ask John McCain to keep his promise and vote to end the
death tax."

Now that the viewers are in a learning trance, they are taken
back to the start of the ad, as though the rest of the ad never happened. In this trance they are given a task in the immediate present and the near future: "Ask John McCain to keep his promise."

At the same time, the ad uses future pacing to throw McCain
and his followers into the future. He must keep his promise because all of his supporters will be counting on him. The emo-
tional/irrational mind will "understand" that he was smiling at the
beginning of the ad because he kept his promise. That's the future
we can imagine. Now, the ad says, we have to go back and make
sure that future happens.

[Picture of McCain smiling zooms in, so his face is closer to us.
On top of the image are the words *Tell him it's important....*]

"Tell John McCain it's important."

[Picture of McCain smiling zooms in more, so he is even closer.
On top of the image are the words *Tell him we're watching....*]

"Tell him we're watching."

[Picture of McCain zooms in again, even closer. On top
of the image are the words *Tell him we'll **remember**....*]

"Tell him we'll remember."

This is pacing used both to create a trance and to modify the
future. The visual effect of the same picture zooming in, closer
and closer, enhances the trance that the viewer is already in. In
this trance the viewer is given more commands. The commands
appear to be directed to McCain ("Tell him") but are also directed
to the viewer—"remember." The ad wants viewers to remember

how McCain votes on the estate tax and to base their support on how he votes. And, as a powerful and useful side benefit, it directs viewers to emotionally anchor the "IRS death tax" with powerful negative states for their own future.

The ad is a direct attempt to change the future by modifying the behavior of a candidate—and the electorate. The target of the ad—like my Texan in the Crown Room—was John McCain himself. If McCain votes against the tax, he will get support. If he votes for the tax, viewers will "remember" and vote against him. The outcome is assured by the ad itself, which has put its viewers into a trance and directed them to take those steps—including the viewer named John McCain, who is imagining all those other people out there looking at him and wondering about the...er... size of his vote.

Just in case you are interested, the ad worked. The ad appeared in May 2006. On June 8, 2006, John McCain voted to bring bill H.R. 8, advocating abolishing the estate tax, to a vote.

FRAMING YOUR WORLDVIEW

If all that the "death tax" ad had done was use future pacing to throw McCain and his supporters into a future in which he supported abolishing the estate tax, it would have been effective. If the ad had done that and also put viewers into a learning trance so they would "remember" how McCain voted, it would have been effective. Both those effects, however, would have had a direct political impact only on John McCain. The ad would have been a powerful tool to change McCain's vote, and no more.

But this ad did something more. It told viewers how to think about the estate tax. It told them to "remember" that the estate tax is an "IRS death tax." That's a powerful frame.

In the first part of this book, we talked about how we know the world through our senses. We remember through pictures, sounds, tastes, and touch. We then sort those sensations through our feelings. That's the brain's folder system. It's not easy to distill the very complex world around us down to these very simple elements, but that's what we have to do because that's how the brain works. We move from complexity to simplicity by using frames.

A *frame* is a simple way of understanding a complex set of feelings and sensations. "My family" is a frame I use to think about the people with whom I have a very particular kind of deep and complex relationship, largely based on love but also on interdependence and mutual support. The frame doesn't actually tell other people anything about who is in my family. I may think my family includes only my wife and children, or I may think of my family as an "extended family" that includes my mother, my in-laws, my siblings, and so forth. It may even include deceased relatives, like my father and my grandparents. For some people "my family" includes people who are not related to them by blood or marriage—they have become family by virtue of close and lasting ties.

A frame won't tell you about any particular content. If we speak of the frame "my family," it won't tell you who I think is in my family, and it won't tell me who you think is in your family. What a frame will disclose, however, and very powerfully, is how to think about a certain set of people. When people say, "My dog is a member of my family," we understand immediately the strong feelings those people must have for their dog. They don't have to explain those feelings at all. They just have to use the word *family* and we get it. That's because "my family" is a frame we all understand at a visceral level, even though its content is highly variable.

Politics is all about frames. When I was in high school, the debating instructor would talk about the importance of framing an argument. He'd say, "How do you frame an argument? What position are you taking? How is that position—that frame—constructed?" He knew that once you've defined a frame, you've colored or changed the meaning of everything that is contained in that frame.

Democrats have finally gotten wise to the power of framing, largely through the work of George Lakoff, a linguistics professor and the author of *Don't Think of an Elephant: Know Your Values and Frame the Debate—The Essential Guide for Progressives.* Before Lakoff, Democrats thought that the best way to frame an argument was to describe the argument as accurately as possible. They thought that you convinced people by talking about content. What Lakoff taught them—and what the conservatives already knew from having listened to people like Newt Gingrich and Frank Luntz and Karl Rove—was that what matters is our *feelings* about the content. Remember: feeling comes first.

Back in part II of this book, we discussed anchors and the way that one word can trigger a feeling. Frames are powerful because they can quickly bring up a whole set of feelings. When we communicate, frames give us a simple way to elicit a particular response to what can be a very complex issue or idea.

The conservatives' "death tax" frame is a perfect example.

THE FRAME ON TAXES

John McCain upset conservatives because of the position he took on the inheritance or estate tax.

The United States was founded in opposition to a monarchy supported by a landed aristocracy. Our country's Founders wanted to make sure that their radical idea—a country governed by We the People—would never be replaced by a king and a bunch of nobles.

Writing more than two hundred years ago, Thomas Jefferson argued for a tax on accumulated wealth because he knew that if wealth was passed down from one generation to the next, those lucky inheritors would turn into new aristocrats. You don't hear about the Founders passing on fortunes because most of them didn't believe in doing so. Thomas Jefferson himself died in debt.

Despite Jefferson's warnings about the danger to "the state" of the accumulation of "excessive wealth," such a tax was not actually put into place until 1916. The estate tax was one of the many reforms put into place during the Progressive Era, a period from 1896 to 1918 when ordinary people rose up against the robber barons and monopolists who had created an aristocracy of wealth, power, and privilege in this country. President Theodore Roosevelt, a Republican, advocated for the estate tax in 1906, arguing, "The man of great wealth owes a particular obligation to the State because he derives special advantages from the mere existence of government."

Teddy Roosevelt, in that simple sentence, gave us the liberal frame on the estate tax and in fact on all taxes. Taxes are the means we use to fund our society, which includes the government institutions that make it possible for people to accumulate wealth.

I often talk to people on my radio show who say they shouldn't have to pay taxes.

"Why not?" I ask them.

"Well, I'm a self-made man," they reply. "I've earned all of my money by starting my own business, and I don't see why I should pay any of it to the government." That's the conservative core story, that self-interest trumps the public interest.

"Okay," I say. "Well, do you have plumbing and electricity in your business?"

"Of course."

"Do your employees and customers use the highway and street system to drive to your business or take public transportation to get there?"

"Of course."

"Okay. And do you use money for your transactions and keep that money in a bank that you trust?"

"Yes."

"Well," I say, "it seems to me you've relied pretty heavily on the government institutions and government-built infrastructure of our society to build your business. You've used public utilities and the public transportation infrastructure; you rely on the public regulation of banking and finance; you probably also are relying on public education to train the people who work for you and on public programs like Social Security and Medicare to cut the cost to you of employee benefits. Seems to me like you owe society a pretty large bill for all the services you use to make your business possible and profitable, and the way we pay that debt is through taxes."

That's the traditional liberal American story on taxes, and it's a powerful one. It works even better for the estate tax.

ESTATE TAX OR DEATH TAX?

Most of us would like to be able to pass along enough money to our children to ensure that they will be able to put food on the table and perhaps even to avoid working for a living for a few generations. We don't, however, want to create a permanent overclass in America simply because someone got lucky and had a very good businessman for a grandfather or a very good investor for a grandmother. Family dynasties—in our day, the Rockefellers, Kennedys, and Bushes spring to mind—are ultimately not healthy for democracy and largely didn't even exist in this nation until after the Civil War, when incorporation and taxation laws were changed to allow the massive accumulation of wealth using the corporate form.

Nor are they healthy for capitalism. Many wealthy businesspeople believe that a powerful class composed mostly of people of inherited wealth cripples innovation and ingenuity, creating a disincentive to work among the best educated. Warren Buffet is a good example of a self-made man who has decided to give his massive estate away rather than give it to his children (the kids don't become paupers—they each will inherit millions).

He's in good company, which includes the father of Bill Gates as well as businessman Bill Foster, who will owe the tax.

"The proponents of estate tax repeal are fond of calling it the 'death tax.' It's not a death tax; it's a rich kids' tax," Foster has said. "The estate tax is one of our time-tested and best tools in preventing the aristocracy of an 'Old Europe' from establishing itself on our shores."[4]

Understood as an inheritance tax or, as Foster calls it, a "rich kids' tax," this tax makes sense. An inheritance tax is a kind of tax even a Republican might be willing to support. And that posed a problem for conservatives, who, as I argue in my previous book, *Screwed: The Undeclared War Against the Middle Class,* actually want to create a new aristocracy. So they changed the frame.

The frame "inheritance tax or estate tax" gave people the positive message that We the People helped create the wealth of the rich, and We the People have a right to use some of that wealth to pay for the institutions that keep our nation strong. It reminded people of the aristocrats of old Britain and of how in America we have a democracy rather than an aristocracy.

The conservatives replaced that nice but not-very-powerful frame "estate tax" with a new frame: "death tax." *Death* is one of Gingrich's anchor words. No one wants to die. It also reminds us that this tax is levied when a loved one dies. Finally, it suggests that everyone will have to pay the tax—because everyone dies—rather than just the 0.27 percent (fewer than three-tenths of 1 percent) of Americans who actually paid it in 2006.[5]

Here's how powerful the frame "death tax" is. When pollsters asked Americans whether they thought the estate tax should be reformed or repealed, 57 percent favored keeping the tax as it was or reforming it, while only 23 percent favored repealing it.[6] When those same pollsters, joined by Frank Luntz's company, later asked voters if the "death tax" was "fair," they got a very different answer: 80 percent of voters polled thought the tax was unfair and should be repealed.[7]

"Death tax" is effective not because it is the best description of the tax. In fact, it is quite misleading. "Death tax" is effective because it triggers a picture of death and raises a whole constellation of negative emotions that arise for us around death. Those negative emotions become anchored to this tax. Once our feelings have changed, the way we think about an idea changes as well. It's an incredibly powerful—albeit deceptive—frame and was promoted in large part by several heirs of the Walton family, who spent millions on front groups that promoted the "IRS death tax" frame to save those few people tens of billions of dollars when their estates move to their heirs.

FIGHTING FRAMES WITH FRAMES

When you come face-to-face with a negative but powerful frame, the best solution usually is to reframe it. Our society communicates through frames, so if you want to change a particular frame, you must offer a different but equally or more powerful frame in its place.

The frame of attention deficit disorder (ADD), for example, tells kids that they are defective, disordered, and diseased. In my opinion that doesn't help children at all. It gives them a disempowering message that they are victims of a disorder and that only the medical field holds the answers or cure for them. (In this regard, though, it's a very useful and profitable frame for the pharmaceutical and psychiatric industries.)

Instead of accepting the ADD frame, I decided to create a new frame to describe this particular constellation of behaviors in a positive way.[8] I suggested that ADD is a vestigial survival mechanism. ADD suits a person living in a hunter-gatherer world, but it puts a person at a disadvantage in a farming or industrial world. For the first few hundred thousand years of human history, I suggested, people with this group of behaviors ruled the land and sea, as hunters, gatherers, and warriors. Now that most of the world's population lives in agricultural or industrial societies, ADD becomes a disadvantage—unless you can reinvent your life to work well as a modern variation on being a hunter-gatherer.

In this hunter-versus-farmer frame, the emphasis on "difference" is taken off the individual person and put onto society. Society changed, and when it did, people with a different set of behaviors—the farmers—were better adapted than the hunters. This change was not necessarily for the better. We live in a world where forty-five thousand people die every day from starvation, where more than a hundred species go extinct every day, where toxic and radioactive waste is sold as fertilizer and sprayed on crops, and where children work in factories for just a few dollars a week. Many of us look at society and wonder why we are being asked to adapt to it rather than asking society to change and adapt to us.

Once children who are distracted, impulsive risk-takers see themselves as hunter-gatherers, their whole sense of self changes. Instead of being dissed with disease, disability, and disorder, they feel empowered to investigate their unique attributes. They can be taught to take advantage of their difference by finding places in our current society where those attributes remain useful. Many entrepreneurs, salespeople, actors, stockbrokers, politicians, cops, and talk-radio hosts have these attributes and use them to their advantage. And in my most recent book on the topic, *The Edison Gene,* I report on how the world's leading geneticists have now tested and *proven* my hypothesis as good science.

WAR VERSUS OCCUPATION

Some frames can be hard to see or hear. When George W. Bush sent troops into Iraq, he told the American people we were at war. That seemed to be a fact, not a frame.

"War," however, is a frame, and it's one of the most powerful in our culture. In the case of Iraq, using the "war" frame was the way that Bush, Rove, and their cronies helped persuade Americans that they were pursuing a noble strategy. Few Americans like to oppose a president when the country is at war.

The fact, however, is that the war in Iraq ended on May 1, 2003, when George W. Bush stood below a "Mission Accomplished" sign aboard the USS *Abraham Lincoln* and correctly declared that we had "victoriously" defeated the Iraqi army and overthrown its government.

Our military machine is tremendously good at fighting wars—blowing up infrastructure, killing opposing armies, and toppling governments. We did that successfully in Iraq, in a matter of a few weeks. We destroyed its army, wiped out its air defenses, devastated its Republican Guard, seized its capital, arrested its leaders, and took control of its government. We won the war.

After we won the war, however, we stayed in Iraq. That is called an *occupation*.

The distinction between the "war" frame and the "occupation" frame is politically critical because wars can be won or lost but occupations most honorably end by redeployments.

We won World War II, and it carried the legacy of Franklin D. Roosevelt to great political heights. We lost the Vietnam War, and it politically destroyed Lyndon B. Johnson, Richard Nixon, and Gerald Ford.

Americans don't like to lose or draw at a war. Even people who oppose wars find it uncomfortable, at some level, to lose; and Republican strategists have used this psychological reality for political gain. When wars are won—even when they're totally illegal and undeclared wars, like Reagan's adventure in Grenada— it tends to create a national good feeling.

On the other hand, when arguably just wars, or at least legally defensible "police action" wars, like Korea, are not won, they wound the national psyche. And losing a war—like the German loss of WWI—can be so psychologically devastating to a citizenry that it sets up a nation for a strongman dictatorship to "restore the national honor."

When using the "war" frame, it's not politically possible to push to end the war: losing a war is too psychologically damaging. When using the frame of "occupation," however, it is very possible to push to end the occupation, and in fact that end is welcomed. In this case, how you frame the U.S. troop presence in Iraq has everything to do with how soon that troop presence ends.

Here's a scenario—fictitious—of how Democrats could have played out the change of frames:

> **TIM RUSSERT:** So, Senator Reid, what do you think of this most recent news from the war in Iraq?
>
> **SENATOR HARRY REID:** The war ended in May 2003, Tim. Our military did its usual brilliant job, and we defeated Saddam's army. The occupation of Iraq, however, isn't going so well, in large part because the Bush administration has totally botched the job, leading to the death of thousands of our soldiers and dragging our nation into disrepute around the world. I'd like to see us greatly scale down the current occupation of Iraq, redeploy our occupation forces to nearby nations in case we're needed by the new Iraqi government, and get our brave young men and women out of harm's way. Occupations have a nasty way of fomenting civil wars, you know, and we don't want this one to go any further than it has.
>
> **TR:** But isn't the war in Iraq part of the global "War on Terror"?
>
> **SR:** Our occupation of Iraq is encouraging more Muslims around the world to eye us suspiciously. Some may even be inspired by our occupation of this Islamic nation to take up arms or unconventional weapons against us, perhaps even here at home, just as Osama bin Laden said he hit us on 9/11 because we were occupying part of his homeland, Saudi Arabia, at the Prince Sultan Air Base, where Bush Sr. first put troops in 1991 to project force into Kuwait and enforce the Iraqi no-fly zone. The Bush policy of an unending occupation of Iraq is increasing the danger that people will use the tactic of terror against us and our allies; and, just as George W. Bush wisely redeployed our troops

from Saudi Arabia, we should begin right now to redeploy our troops who are occupying Iraq.

TR: But the war...

SR: Tim, Tim, Tim! The war is over! George W. Bush declared victory himself, in May 2003, when our brave soldiers seized control of Iraq. That's the definition of the end of a war, as anybody who's ever served in the military can tell you. Unfortunately, our occupation of Iraq since the end of the war, using a small military force and a lot of Halliburton, hasn't worked. We should take Halliburton's billions and give them to the Iraqis so they can rebuild their own nation—the way we helped Europeans rebuild after World War II—and go from being an occupying power to being an ally of Iraq and the Iraqi people, like we did with Japan and Germany.

TR [bewildered]: I can't call it a war anymore? We have to change our NBC "War in Iraq" banners and graphics?

SR [patting Russert's hand]: Yes, Tim. The war is over. It's now an occupation and has been for three years. And like all occupations, it's best to wrap it up so Iraq can get on with its business. I'm sure your graphics people can come up with some new logos that say "Occupation of Iraq." It'll be a nice project for them, maybe even earn them some much-needed overtime pay. The "War in Iraq" graphics are getting a bit stale, don't you think? After all, soon we'll be able to say that we fought World War II in less time than we've been in Iraq. Wars are usually short, but occupations—particularly when they're done stupidly—can be hellish.

TR [brightening]: Ah, so! Now I get it! I even wrote about wars and occupations in my book about my dad. Thanks for coming on the program today and clarifying this for us.

Frames matter and have consequences, sometimes life-and-death consequences. If the Democrats had been able to shift the media's discussion from "war" to "occupation" back in 2003, we could have prevented the deaths of many, many Iraqis and thousands of U.S. soldiers.

PART IV

THE MAP IS NOT THE TERRITORY

CHAPTER 11

LEARNING
THE LEGEND

*We are not afraid to entrust the American people with unpleasant
facts, foreign ideas, alien philosophies, and competitive values.
For a nation that is afraid to let its people judge the truth and
falsehood in an open market is a nation that is afraid of its people.*

— JOHN F. KENNEDY

In part II of this book, you learned how the brain processes senses
into feelings and feelings into thoughts. In part III you learned that
we can guide those feelings through techniques like anchoring, future pacing, the learning trance, and framing. With each code you
crack, you have moved from being an unconscious communicator
to a conscious one and from being an incompetent communicator
to a competent one.

The next and last step to cracking the code is to become an
unconsciously competent communicator. As such you will master
the *art* of political persuasion as well as the *science*. Once you master this last section of the communication code, you will move
from being able to persuade the person sitting next to you to being
able to persuade large groups of people.

When we move from persuading a single individual to the
much larger and more complex task of political persuasion, we
need a whole new set of tools. Unconscious competence requires
understanding not only *how* the communication code works but
also *why* it works. Without understanding the why, even competent communicators can fail to persuade. The abortion debates of

141

the 1980s and 1990s provide a useful example of two competent attempts at communication around the same issue and why one worked better than the other.

PRO-LIFE OR PRO-CHOICE?

Through the 1980s and 1990s, one of the defining issues for both liberals and conservatives in the United States was abortion. Republicans had trouble winning elections if they were in favor of a woman's being able to decide whether or not to have an abortion. Democrats had trouble winning elections if they were against a woman's right to choose to have an abortion. The abortion debate provided voters and pundits with a kind of litmus test.

As an issue, abortion naturally triggers deep-seated feelings, and the word *abortion* itself triggers mainly negative emotions. How we feel about a word or an idea largely determines how we think about it. Because the word *abortion* is such a powerful negative anchor, advocates of legalizing abortion needed a different way to talk about this issue that affects women and their bodies. In 1973, just after *Roe v. Wade* made abortion legal, feminists found the frame they had been looking for: "pro-choice."[1]

This was a time in America's history when women were demanding the right to be treated as equals to men under the law. Even though American women won the vote in 1920, many laws were still stacked against women. It was not until 1963 that women won the right to equal pay for equal work (Equal Pay Act), 1964 that women won the right to not face discrimination in the workplace (Civil Rights Act), and 1965 that married women won the right to legally use contraception (*Griswold v. Connecticut*). The rallying cry of the feminist movement in the 1960s and early 1970s was that women were equals to men and had the right to choose what to make of their lives and what to do with their own bodies.

"Pro-choice" was a potent frame for those who felt strongly about a woman's right to equality with men. The frame "pro-choice" appeals at a gut level to anyone who believes that all people have certain inalienable rights. It's a frame that ties directly into the words of this country's Founders, who declared that each of us has the right to life, liberty, and the pursuit of happiness.

Within a year after the "pro-choice" frame appeared in print in 1975, however, opponents of legalizing abortion struck back with a frame of their own: "pro-life." "Pro-life" had for years been the frame used extensively by the mainly liberal anti–death penalty movement. Abortion opponents took that "pro-life" frame and repurposed it as a "forced pregnancy" frame.

Both "pro-choice" and "pro-life" are strong frames. Yet a woman's right to choose whether or not to have an abortion, when, and under what circumstances, has been decaying since *Roe v. Wade*. More than forty states now have a ban on late-term abortions.[2] In thirty-three states, teenagers cannot obtain a legal abortion without parental consent or parental notification.[3] The number of U.S. abortion providers declined by 11 percent between 1996 and 2000 (from 2,042 to 1,819). Eighty-seven percent of all U.S. counties lacked an abortion provider in 2000. These counties were home to 34 percent of all 15- to 44-year-old women.[4] In the battle of the frames, "pro-life" is winning. Why?

UNDERSTANDING THE WHY

In part III we talked about how the meaning of a communication is the response you get: what matters is not what I say but what my listener thinks I said. We talked about ways to make sure that my listener would get my meaning. That's one key to the communication code.

What we didn't talk much about, however, is why communication works this way. Why don't other people see or hear or feel the world the same way I do? Don't we all see, hear, and feel the same things? If we walk into a room with a desk and a chair, don't we all see a desk? If we sit down, don't we all feel the same padded cushion?

The answer, in short, is no. We don't. We don't all see exactly the same thing, and we don't all feel that cushion in exactly the same way. There really is a desk and a chair in the room, but each of us experiences that desk and chair differently.

Let me give you an example from my own life. I live on a houseboat on a river. That's the territory I live in. "Territory" can be used to describe any part of the physical world. A room with a desk and a chair is a territory, for example. And "territory" can also be used to describe our psychological and political worlds (more on that shortly).

I can describe to you where I live—my territory—even if you are not here with me. Right now, sitting in my houseboat, looking at the river, I can tell you that the water is brown/blue/greenish, there are ripples, there are ducks along the bank, and so forth. My description of the river becomes a *map* of the territory for you. You are not experiencing the territory yourself, but you can experience my map of it.

Now, what happens if you come to visit me? What if you and I are standing on my dock, looking at the river together?

We are looking at the same territory, the river. We both can see the blue heron fishing on the riverbank, feel the cool-water breeze, and smell and hear the water as it flows around the pilings on which our dock and home float up and down with the tides. We can discuss the river and share what we each see and hear and feel. But here's a secret that most of us know but never really accept. It's the secret that will make you an unconsciously competent communicator:

Even though we are both experiencing the same territory, our individual experience of that territory will always remain different.

When we both stand and look at the river together, we both notice and *experience* different things. I might be knowledgeable about trees and see beech trees and willows, whereas you see just trees. You might like to fish and will know where they're most likely to be found, seeing those places that I don't even know exist.

We also come with different emotions that change how we understand our sensory experiences. I might have memories of this river that color my feelings about it and how I see it—and those are memories and feelings that are different from yours. Your experience of rivers in the past is certainly different from mine. Because our senses are tied to our emotions and memories, and mediated by our individual nervous systems, we will never see or hear or smell or taste or feel things in exactly the same way as another person.

We already know this. One of our kids loves peppermint ice cream; the other kid hates it. Same ice cream, different experience.

One person listens to a Beethoven symphony and hears patterns of sound; another hears a story; another is bored and tunes out.

We have these experiences of our differences among each other all the time. It's what makes life so rich and interesting.

Those differences have significant consequences, however, for communication. Anytime we communicate, we are never going to be successful at giving people a pure experience of objective reality—the territory.

No matter how well I describe my river to you, my map of the territory will never match your map of the territory. And neither map *is* the territory!

Distortion, Deletion, Generalization

There is a reason why our maps usually don't match up. We put our sensory experience of the world through three different kinds of filters: *distortion, deletion,* and *generalization.* Our brain instantaneously and continuously uses these filters to be more efficient in our communication and our experience of the world.

As you read this book, you are engaged in these three kinds of filters. Until you read this sentence, you were probably not aware of what is on the wall to your left or the temperature in the room. You *deleted* that experience—and you will delete it again by the time this chapter is over—because our minds simply can't process more than five to nine things at once.

You're also *distorting* your experiences right now. In distortion we misrepresent parts of reality, often as a way of simplifying experience. We almost always distort our memories of events because we file those events in ways that make the most emotional sense to us (remember the Pentaflex folders) rather than according to what our senses actually told us at the time.

We also distort and generalize when we make assumptions about others. You may have made a whole set of assumptions about what was in this book when you read the title, *Cracking the Code*, or when you saw that "Thom Hartmann, Air America Radio host" was the author, or that I was on a Vermont roster of psychotherapists and once was the executive director of a residential treatment facility for abused and emotionally disturbed children, or that I was an advertising industry executive and consultant, or that I'm the author of more than twenty books and an entrepreneur, or that I did international relief work on and off for more than twenty years on five continents in several war and conflict zones, or that Louise and I have been married for thirty-five years and have three grown children and four cats, or that doing all of these things pretty easily qualifies me as a poster child for attention deficit disorder. Each evokes a frame, and each frame is filled with shorthand distortions, deletions, and generalizations.

You've also been *generalizing* your experience of the place you are in as you read this book. We don't have enough time or energy to analyze every object we see that has four legs. We generalize and say to ourselves, *that is a chair, this is a table.* Right now you may be aware that you are in a room, or on a plane, or wherever you happen to be, but you are not paying attention to all of the details that make up the place you are in. You did not spend time thinking about the floor, the walls, or the objects in the room before you decided that you were in a room. To get through life, most of the time we have to label the world around us without thinking about its specificity.

Deletion, distortion, and generalization are necessary filters that enable us to process and make sense of the tremendous amount of information available to our senses. Yet when using these filters, we also sometimes delete, distort, or generalize in ways that may not be appropriate or useful. We may lose information we need, or we may misapprehend information.

When I tell you about the river I am looking at, my map of the territory has been filtered through my deletion, distortion, and generalization process into language. That is, the map I describe to you is already not the territory. It's just a generalized and distorted version of *my* map, filled with deletions and handed to you in the form of words. (Forgot to mention that eagle in the tree on the riverbank, didn't I?)

When I communicate that map to you, I communicate through language. That language is then filtered by you through your own internal deletion, distortion, and generalization process into *your* map. Your map is, in turn, a deleted, distorted, and generalized version of my map, which is in turn a deleted, distorted, and generalized version of the territory.

You may think when I describe the river to you that you are getting the territory, but you're not. All we can ever get from another person is a deleted, distorted, and generalized version of their map.

MAP VERSUS TERRITORY

Let's make the metaphor solid and talk about a Rand McNally highway map. As children learn in grammar school, a map's code is necessary to read and make sense of a map. That code is called the *legend*. It's a nice metaphor, *legend*, because the map's code really is the story of the map, and it tells us how the map was created.

For example, if I am going to drive from Chicago to Ames, Iowa, I will look at my road map, which will show me which roads to take. But if I want to know what kind of roads they will be, I have to look at the legend, which will let me know that expressways are red, highways are bolded black, and 2-lane country roads are thin black lines.

If I want to know how long the journey will take, I have to consult the legend again, which may tell me that 1 inch on the map equals 50 miles. I can measure the inches, multiply by 50, divide by my driving speed (which I won't reveal here!), and figure out how long it will take me to get from Chicago to Ames.

Geographers study the stories that maps tell. They can discern how people think about their world by the kinds of maps they make. Christopher Columbus, for example, had a map of the world in which Europe was at the center, and all the places he visited were "discoveries" because they had never been known to Europeans before. The people living in those places had their own maps, telling themselves stories about the relationships between their people and the many other people who they knew lived on the land. For them the Europeans were a discovery that necessitated new maps. And for every culture in the world, the center of its map was the center of its living space (so much so that during the Middle Ages in Europe, people who suggested that the Earth wasn't at the center of the universe were put to death).

Think about how you would map your neighborhood. One map is the satellite map, showing how your home looks from outer space. Another is a road map of your city or county that shows all the streets near you but doesn't show your house at all. A third map is the computer map your friend uses to get to your house, which may show streets or may be just a list of directions. A fourth map is the map of real estate values, which becomes very important when you want to sell your house. A fifth map is the map you carry around in your head of your neighbors—who lives next to you, who lives across the way from you, and so forth. You may even have a map of everyone's dog, if you are a dog owner, or a map of all the playgrounds in the neighborhood if you have young kids.

Which of these maps is the map of the territory? All of them and none of them. Each map engages in deletion, distortion, and generalization. What makes these maps valuable to us isn't whether they accurately represent the territory but how *useful* they are to us. If I don't have kids, I probably don't care where the playgrounds are. If I rent, I probably don't care about real estate values. I may not care what my house looks like from outer space. What matters to us is what story a particular map can tell us—the story of who lives nearby, or what our financial value is, or how someone can find us.

It helps to remember that the code for maps is called a legend. The key to unlocking any map is the story the map tells. That's true for communicative maps as well. What matters isn't how accurate the map is—because no map will ever accurately reflect the territory—but rather how *useful* it is.

Making a Choice

It's a challenge to accurately communicate information about the physical world—the world that actually exists. It's an even bigger challenge to communicate about the political world, which is essentially a series of abstractions used to describe processes that have an impact on the real world. The maps we create of these processes are always very different from the territory, which is precisely what is going on in the abortion debate.

What kind of story does the "pro-choice" frame tell? "Pro-choice" tells the story of modern feminism. For hundreds of years, women struggled for the ability to make their own choices. They struggled to own private property. They struggled to get the vote. They struggled for equal pay. "Pro-choice" reminds us that the right to a safe and legal abortion is the next step in that long story of women's struggles for their rights.

That is a very powerful and inspiring story—for liberals. For women who want to assert their rights, and for men who support those women, "pro-choice" is an uplifting reminder that women have succeeded before and can succeed again. For those who embrace this story, it may also remind us of the Founders' struggle to secure from the king of England the rights to life, liberty, and the pursuit of happiness. It may remind us of the Civil Rights Movement and the Gay Liberation Movement and the many other movements of the 1960s that were about giving people the right to choose their destiny.

"Pro-choice," in short, is a very powerful story for people who already believe in women's right to equality with men and thus their right to decide whether they want to have access to a safe and legal abortion. The task of this particular frame, however, is not just to mobilize progressives who already support *Roe v. Wade* but to persuade those who are undecided or opposed to abortion rights. In that, the frame fails.

The main reason why it fails is because conservatives tell a very different story about the 1960s leading up to the 1973 *Roe v. Wade* Supreme Court decision. For them that era marked a time when the country lost its moral compass. Their story about America is not one of progress but one of decay. The source of their motivation, as we discuss in the next chapter, is fear rather than hope. So a story about hope doesn't speak to them.

Many conservatives also don't hold as a primary value the idea of living in a society in which everyone has choices. They believe in the dominator model—that some people should be the "deciders" and that others should do what the "deciders" say. Con servatives who are members of the religious right in particular tend to believe that men are the deciders and that women should abide by their decisions.

For example, I did my radio program live from the Republican National Convention in New York in 2004. A leading proponent of forced pregnancy sat in front of me and said that abortion at any time, under any circumstances, was murder.

"Isn't it a capital crime to commission murder?" I asked.

"It is," he said. "Women who hire an abortion doctor are just as guilty."

"Well," I said, "the penalty for murder, or hiring murder, is death in many states. Do you think women who have abortions should be executed by hanging, by firing squad, by lethal injection, or by gas chamber?"

Without missing a beat, he said, "That's up to the states to decide what method of execution they are going to use."

Choice, for him, is a symptom of what is wrong with this country. The "pro-choice" frame is not a map that is useful to conservatives.

On the other hand (and ironically), the framing words that conservatives chose for the abortion debate make a lot of sense to liberals.

The conservatives chose to frame their support for legally enforced pregnancies as "pro-life." "Pro-life" tells a much simpler story than "pro-choice." The "pro-life" frame tells us that every single human being is valuable, which is a very positive message. And it suggests that the world is divided into two kinds of people: those who are pro-life and those who are pro-death. It's not hard to choose which side anybody would rather be on, particularly after the anti–death penalty movement had used the "pro-life" frame for more than a century.

Now, you may say, hold on, the conservatives' map is not accurate. The same people who say they are "pro-life" about abortion are often in favor of the death penalty; many were in favor of the war in Iraq, and some don't even care if the life of the pregnant mother is at risk because of the pregnancy. The forced-pregnancy crowd may be a minority, but they are loud enough to appear numerous.

This highlights how the effectiveness of a map is based on usefulness, not accuracy, in part because no map is totally accurate.

If I'm trying to drive to my friend's house, it doesn't help me to have a map of the real estate values on the block or of the location of kids' playgrounds. I'd be better off with directions that delete, distort, and generalize about those things so long as the map does tell me what street my friend lives on.

The conservatives' forced-pregnancy map deletes the many situations in which its proponents actually favor death. It distorts the many side effects of their position, one of which is that some women will die if abortion is not safe and legal. It generalizes from one particular medical procedure to a broad worldview. It implicitly embraces the notion that women are weak and emotionally and mentally inferior to men and thus in need of the protection and the guidance of men (and, by proxy, government run by men). Neither the "pro-life" nor the "pro-choice" map accurately represents the complex and multifaceted terrain of the abortion issue.

The "pro-life" frame succeeds as a map, however, because it modifies the territory in a very powerful way. Whereas the "pro-choice" frame suggests only that people who are opposed to abortion are opposed to women having choices, the "pro-life" frame suggests that people in favor of a woman's having access to safe and legal abortions are also in favor of murder.

The "pro-life" frame suggests that anyone who does not embrace pro-life supports death. Because no one supports death, they must, de facto, support life and thus be against abortion. Once you get into the "pro-life" frame and accept the pro-life story, there is no way out, no room for discussion.

The pro-life map is accurate only for those whose territory is defined by certain religious or social perspectives, but it is *useful* for them. The same can be said for the pro-choice map. The story is all in the telling. Those who control the map will define and ultimately control the territory. In fact, the map is more than just useful. The pro-life map actually controls the story.

CHAPTER 12

THE MOTIVATION CODE

You gain strength, courage, and confidence by every
experience in which you really stop to look fear in the face.
You must do the thing which you think you cannot do.

— ELEANOR ROOSEVELT

In the spring of 2007, France was preparing for the most important national election in many years, an election people believed would decide the direction of their country for years to come. The two candidates who made it to the final round represented the right and left wings of French politics. Nicolas Sarkozy, the candidate of the Union for a Popular Movement, and Ségolène Royal, the candidate of the Socialist Party.

Compared with American politicians, Sarkozy and Royal may seem more alike than different. Both, for example, support what conservatives here would call "big government." In their worldviews, however, these two French politicians are completely different, and they used very different motivational strategies for their listeners.

Speaking at a celebration of his first-round voting victory, Sarkozy spoke of his deepest aspiration: "I want to tell all the French who are scared, who are scared of the future, who feel fragile, vulnerable, who find life harder and harder, I want to tell them that I want to protect them."[1]

Royal, by contrast, speaking on the same day to her supporters, said that she wanted to "lead the fight for change, so that France can stand up again, to get optimism back."[2]

In these two voices, we hear the conservative and liberal stories: the conservative story that the world is an evil place where we must be protected, and the liberal story that the world is a good place where we can achieve our fullest aspirations. The aim of these two speeches, however, was not just for the politicians to convey their core stories. Each politician was aiming to motivate voters to choose him or her on election day.

Sarkozy chose to motivate his listeners by reminding them what they wanted to leave behind: I know you are afraid of pain, he said, but if you vote for me, I will protect you; you will be able to leave that fear and pain behind.

Royal chose to motivate her listeners by reminding them of what they wanted to move toward: I know you want more from this country, she said, and if you vote for me, I will lead you into a brighter future where your wishes will be fulfilled.

Toward pleasure or away from pain, toward hope or away from fear—mentally and emotionally we never stand still. We are always doing one of two things: either moving toward something we want or moving away from something we don't want. We are always moving toward pleasure or away from pain, and we develop and use strategies that include both of these to motivate ourselves and others.

The Moving-away-from-pain Strategy

In the short run, the most effective strategy for persuasive communication is to motivate someone to *move away from pain*. The reason is simple: it's physiological. If you get an electric shock, you pull your finger out of the wall socket. If you're barefoot and step on glass, you lift up your foot. "Wow!" "Gotta do something!"

Causing people to experience or even imagine pain gets an immediate response.

Moving-away-from-pain strategies are very powerful because they're among the first we learn as children. Many children's first spoken word is "No!" because they so strongly experienced parental admonishments to avoid pain: "No, don't pull on the tablecloth!" "No, don't touch the hot stove!" "No, don't go near the street!" And by the age of two, most children have experienced enough pain, accidental or unintentionally self-inflicted, that they know well the association between "No!" and pain or the threat of pain.

As adults we internalize these moving-away-from-pain strategies and use them to motivate ourselves and others. Dick Cheney motivated voters using the pain strategy when he suggested that if Americans voted for Democrats, terrorists would attack the United States. Vote for Democrats, feel pain. Vote for Republicans, avoid pain. (Similarly, in 1998, Osama bin Laden said that if we didn't remove our soldiers from Saudi Arabia's Prince Sultan Air Base, where we'd positioned them in 1991 for the Gulf War, he would attack us for defiling the Holy Land. We didn't, and he did.)

The downside of the moving-away-from-pain strategy is that over time it stops working or produces terribly dysfunctional results. It's like whipping a horse to keep it going. At first it works, but after a while if you keep whipping the horse over and over, harder and harder, eventually the horse will drop dead of exhaustion, or it will give up and stop trying to avoid the pain and just sit there and whimper. When overused, the moving-away-from-pain strategy eventually becomes ineffective.

THE MOVING-TOWARD-PLEASURE STRATEGY

At the other end of the motivational spectrum is *moving toward pleasure.*

Pleasure is typically nowhere near as extreme as pain. Prick your finger with a pin: it's hard to produce an experience of pleasure that is as strong and as brief as that common experience of pain. Probably the closest we get to such feelings of pleasure are either drug-induced experiences (studies with rats show that they'll push a bar to get cocaine until they starve to death)[3] or sexual orgasm (which will cause humans and other animals to risk their lives on occasion).

But broadly, setting aside drug-induced and sexual ones, the vast majority of our moving-toward-pleasure behaviors are very gentle and subtle. Getting a pay raise, having a good conversation, or enjoying a nice lunch—none of that, in terms of the intensity of the sensation, comes even close to the short-term power of the experience of having somebody poke your finger with a pin. If somebody pokes you, you'll jump immediately. But most of us have never involuntarily jumped for a meal or a nice conversation.

Moving toward pleasure is like the natural force of gravity. Just as gravity is the weakest of the natural forces, it is also the most steady and constant. It's keeping you and me glued to our seats. It steadily acts through our lives, never varying. Although moving-toward-pleasure strategies don't always produce immediate changes in behavior like moving-away-from-pain strategies do, they can last over the long haul, and they can motivate people throughout their entire lives.

Saving up for a house is a moving-toward-pleasure strategy we practice when we are young adults. We could rent all our lives, but we look forward to homeownership. It's the same with saving for a college education for your kids or for a special vacation. In public life we invest money in schools because we look forward to the bright, well-educated workers and citizens those schools will produce. All of these are moving-toward-pleasure strategies.

How the Motivation Code Works

How do we motivate ourselves? How do we motivate other people? Anyone who has ever tried to diet knows that motivation is not as easy as it seems, even when you have both strategies (the pleasure of getting thinner and the pain of getting diabetes or heart disease) to motivate you.

Understanding how motivation works leads to two immediate outcomes.

The first is that we can change our own internal motivation systems and decision-making strategies to move ourselves in the directions that we want to move. We begin to more consciously make motivation-based decisions: how to better set goals and how to affect our own present and future behavior.

Second, we have a better handle on, a better view of, and a better story for how to help other people at least understand clearly what it is we're suggesting in a political context so they can decide whether or not to be motivated by it.

And there's a built-in bonus: Once people know how motivational strategies work, when such strategies are being intentionally but surreptitiously inflicted on them they can spot them coming and internally diffuse them. In other words, it provides us with a defense system.

In my opening example, a conservative used the moving-away-from-pain strategy and a liberal used the moving-toward-pleasure strategy. It makes sense that conservatives, who tend to think that the world is an evil place, would tend toward a moving-away-from-pain strategy; likewise, liberals, who tend to think the world is a good place, tend toward a moving-toward-pleasure strategy.

The fact is, however, that to be maximally competent in the world, we all need to have both types of motivational strategies available to us, both internally to motivate ourselves and externally to motivate others.

We want a safe nation (moving away from the pain of danger) and a nation where every person can fulfill their greatest potential (moving toward the pleasure of fulfillment). From a communication perspective, both types of motivational strategies have their uses.

The Two-strategy Solution

One of the most significant communication problems most people face is that they don't have a lot of flexibility when they're developing internal or external motivational strategies.

Back in 1978 I was the executive director of a residential treatment facility for abused and emotionally disturbed kids in New Hampshire. A majority of the kids who came to us were the victims of severe abuse. But they were also the victims of parents who really had only one tool. They had just one way to accomplish what they wanted to accomplish, and that was using the moving-away-from-pain motivational strategy. It was the only strategy that they understood, and so they would inflict pain on their children to motivate them.

The parents would yell at them when they were very young, and that worked for a little while. But then it stopped working, so then they hit them, and that worked for a little while, and then that stopped working. And then they hit them harder, and that worked for a little while, and then that stopped working. And then they started hitting them with things, and it would escalate to the point where one of the first kids we took in, a little boy named Tony, came to us because his brother had been starved to death by his parents in the basement. He literally died, and his parents insisted they were doing it to try to teach him to behave.

Virtually every severely abusive parent I've ever talked to lacked a complete set of motivational strategies or the ability to use them.

Child abuse may seem like an extreme example, but it's all too typical of the way most of us Americans learn to motivate ourselves.

At the office, managers tend to manage by moving people away from pain. They yell. They bang their fists on the desk. Some CEOs are not-so-secretly admired in the business pages for going on rampages to get what they want. Americans value short-terms gains, so they value a short-term strategy like moving away from pain.

But anyone who has worked in such an environment knows that moving-away-from-pain strategies generally make for lousy management and low morale. It's much more effective to motivate people by offering them pleasure. Carrots work better over the long term than sticks. Good managers understand that their job is to catch people doing things right: if you catch people doing things right, they'll want to do more of it and they'll grow and get better and better.

It's no coincidence that a company that offers its employees health care, organic food in the cafeteria, and on-site child care has posted soaring profits. Google, for example, knows how to motivate its employees toward pleasure and thus gets great productivity. On the other hand, many companies that are in the process of preparing for buyouts or are being managed by people whose compensation is tied to quarterly profits squeeze their employees so hard that very little pleasure is left. In the short term, it produces profit spikes, but over the long term employee turnover and loss of functional corporate culture harm the business.

BE VERY AFRAID: THE BUSH STRATEGY

The Bush Jr. administration, like the parents and the office managers I just discussed, relied primarily on the moving-away-from-pain strategy. Its worldview was so consumed with the idea of an evil that had to be restrained that Bush, Cheney, et al. couldn't imagine any time it would be safe to allow people to move toward pleasure.

Bush's speech in 2004 before the Republican National Convention was a most powerful example of someone using the pain strategy to motivate voters. This is how the speech began:

> Mr. Chairman—Mr. Chairman, delegates, fellow citizens: I am honored by your support, and I accept your nomination for president of the United States. [applause]
>
> When I—when I said those words four years ago, none of us could have envisioned what these years would bring. In the heart of this great city, we saw tragedy arrive on a quiet morning. We saw the bravery of rescuers grow with danger. We learned of passengers on a doomed plane who died with a courage that frightened their killers. [applause]

Why would Bush start a speech with the dangers of 9/11 at a time when most presidents going into their second term would have talked about how much substance they had delivered to the American people and what a bright future they were creating together?

One answer might be that Bush was struggling in the polls all through the summer of 2004. Another was that his war in Iraq was already heading south. Yet he had positive news to share: Millionaires and billionaires were doing better in the United States than at any time since the 1920s.

Even when Bush did try to share the good news, however, he just couldn't leave the pain behind. Here are his comments on the economy:

> My plan begins with providing the security and opportunity of a growing economy. We now compete in a global market that provides new buyers for our goods, but new competition for our workers. To create more jobs in America, America must be the best place in the world to do business. [applause] To create jobs,

my plan will encourage investment and expansion by restraining federal spending, reducing regulation, and making the tax relief permanent. [applause] To create jobs, we will make our country less dependent on foreign sources of energy. [applause] To create jobs, we will expand trade and level the playing field to sell American goods and services across the globe. [applause] And we must protect small business owners and workers from the explosion of frivolous lawsuits that threaten jobs across America. [applause]

Another drag on our economy is the current tax code, which is a complicated mess—filled with special interest loopholes, saddling our people with more than six billion hours of paperwork and headache every year. The American people deserve—and our economic future demands—a simpler, fairer, pro-growth system. [applause] In a new term, I will lead a bipartisan effort to reform and simplify the federal tax code. [applause]

Bush's very first word about the economy here is "security." This new economy mainly benefits the public, it appears, by preventing some danger. What would that danger be, in an economy that Bush himself says is "growing"? Bush proceeds to remind workers that they have lots of competitors now (in part because of Bush's support of "free trade") and reminds us that America is "dependent on foreign sources of energy" (in part because of Bush's embrace of the Saudis and refusal to develop alternative energy sources). Another problem for the American worker, apparently, is "frivolous lawsuits" and the tax code, which "is a complicated mess." If not for the first sentence, anyone reading this part of the speech would think America was facing a deep recession, depression, or worse (and many working-class people probably felt that way). The news was bad, Bush was saying, and only electing him would make it better. It's the classic moving-away-from-pain motivational strategy.

Bush's strategy worked because its aim was to get him reelected, and electoral victories are short-term strategies. Over the long term, of course, Bush lost support, nose-diving to approval ratings below those of Nixon during the Watergate scandal. Bush, like many CEOs, cared only about short-term gain, and now we are left cleaning up the mess he scared us into creating.

Contrast Bush's speech with Franklin D. Roosevelt's "Four Freedoms" speech, given as the State of the Union Address in 1941, just months before the United States entered World War II. The world was not looking very rosy in 1941. The country was only slowly crawling out of the Great Depression. Norway, Belgium, Holland, and France had surrendered to the Nazis; Britain was being blitzed; war was raging across Africa, the Middle East, and all of Europe and was soon to be taken to Asia. The world was not a safe place.

Roosevelt began his speech, like Bush, with thoughts about security. He pointed out that America was in danger. He suggested that Americans might need to restrain that danger to be free. He said:

> No realistic American can expect from a dictator's peace international generosity, or return of true independence, or world disarmament, or freedom of expression, or freedom of religion—or even good business. Such a peace would bring no security for us or for our neighbors. Those who would give up essential liberty to purchase a little temporary safety deserve neither liberty nor safety.

Roosevelt understood the value of moving away from pain. Yet the point of his speech was to insist that a country will remain great only if its primary animus is to move toward the future. It is these words about the future that give the speech its name and make it great. They are worth quoting in full, as we hear so little about the future in our current political communications:

> In the future days which we seek to make secure, we look forward to a world founded upon four essential human freedoms.

The first is freedom of speech and expression—everywhere in the world.

The second is freedom of every person to worship God in his own way—everywhere in the world.

The third is freedom from want, which, translated into world terms, means economic understandings which will secure to every nation a healthy peacetime life for its inhabitants—everywhere in the world.

The fourth is freedom from fear, which, translated into world terms, means a world-wide reduction of armaments to such a point and in such a thorough fashion that no nation will be in a position to commit an act of physical aggression against any neighbor—anywhere in the world.

That is no vision of a distant millennium. It is a definite basis for a kind of world attainable in our own time and generation. That kind of world is the very antithesis of the so-called "new order" of tyranny which the dictators seek to create with the crash of a bomb.

It's relatively easy to create a moving-away-from-pain strategy. Our bodies are primed to "fight or flight." We are wired to know danger and to move away from it right away, without asking any tough questions. Any effective communication will take advantage of this moving-away-from-pain instinct.

Yet we also are wired for pleasure, and it is a deeper and stronger emotion. It endures across years, generations, and ages. We still hold the positive liberal vision of the Founders of this nation. Roosevelt knew that, and that is why, all through the long war with Germany, he reminded Americans that "the only thing we have to fear is fear itself." Fear and pain lead to short-term action, but hope and pleasure are the frames that have always led us to create a new world.

WHICH MOTIVATIONAL STRATEGY?

A Transcript from the Thom Hartmann Program
December 29, 2006

THOM: We have on the phone Loretta in Brooklyn, New York, and Pete in Madison, Wisconsin. Loretta, you have an easy time getting up in the morning?

LORETTA: Oh, I most certainly do.

THOM: Okay, great. And Pete, you have a hard time getting up in the morning?

PETE: Absolutely.

THOM: Okay, great. I have a question for both of you. Let me just start with you, Loretta. Loretta, when you first wake up in the morning, what is the first thing that you typically think of, at least that you're willing to talk about on the radio?

LORETTA: Turning on the computer.

THOM: And are you looking forward to that?

LORETTA: Yes, I do.

THOM: And when you look forward, when you imagine your day, the things that you are going to do throughout your day, broadly, what are you thinking of when you get up in the morning?

LORETTA: Excuse me?

THOM: The other things of your day that you're thinking about?

LORETTA: Oh, I already have my day planned out by the day before.

THOM: Ah, okay. And do you have it planned out based on the things that you are looking forward to doing, or the things that you're trying to avoid doing?

LORETTA: No, I look forward to everything I do.

THOM: Okay. Loretta, hang on just a second here. Pete, when you wake up in the morning, what's the first thing that comes into your mind?

PETE: Well, sometimes it's, "Oh God, I'm awake," but most of the time it's kind of wondering what's going on in the world, in the news that day.

THOM: And what is it that, on a typical day, or this morning if you can remember, what is it that you might have thought about? What motivates you to turn the radio on in the morning?

PETE: Your show; actually, your show is pretty positive. But yeah, that's pretty much what motivates me, is what's going on in the news, and even though I don't like a lot of what's going on and there's the moving away from pain, I want to be involved, so it's almost an approach-avoidance conflict, in a way.

THOM: Yeah, yeah, it sounds like you're actually sort of in the middle area. I had a person—I used to teach this in workshops on marketing, advertising, communication—a person who had a really hard time [waking up]. This guy had three alarm clocks by his bed. He had to because each one only had three opportunities on the snooze button before it gave up, and so he'd go through nine snooze buttons before he finally got up. And I asked him, "What is it that you imagine when you wake up?" and he said, "I think about going into work." And then I said, "What do you think about going into work?" and he said, "Well, I imagine myself showing up late, and that's how I get myself out of bed." And then I said, "Well, and then what do you imagine?" and he says, "And then I imagine myself, you know, being yelled at by my boss." And I said, "What's after that?" and he said, "Well, and then my boss fires me, finally, because I've been late too many times. And then I imagine myself standing in the unemployment line and being humiliated by standing there. And then I imagine the unemployment running out and being kicked out of my apartment."

PETE: Wow.

THOM: "And as I'm being kicked out of my apartment, I'm living under a bridge with all my stuff in a shopping cart and some guy beats me up." And that was literally the movie this guy ran in his mind every morning in order to force himself out of bed. And as we deconstructed it, we learned that, over time, over a period of years, he had gone from a relatively short negative moving-away-from-pain strategy of just "Oh, my god, I'm going to be late for work if I don't get out of bed" all the way through this whole thing of "I'm going to end up dying and homeless and being beat up and rolled by people cause I'm living on the streets" because he had to keep amping up the pain for it to work. And I'm curious, Pete, if you have any parallel experience. You don't need to give us any details on it, but is there any resonance there for you?

PETE: Not quite to the extent that he went to with it, but there is a resonance with regard to not only the political situation but then, you know, sometimes I get into all the, you know, start thinking about the things that are wrong in my life and it sort of branches off from there, basically—short version.

THOM: Yeah, so, right, in other words you wake up thinking, "Oh, this could happen, that could happen, and might as well just stay in bed."

PETE: Yeah, exactly.

THOM: Okay. So, what I would like to suggest, Pete, is that you borrow, or you can even steal it if you prefer, part of Loretta's strategy, if that's okay with you, Loretta?

LORETTA: Oh, definitely.

THOM: So, what I'd like to suggest is, Loretta, your strategy is, before you go to bed at night, you think about the things the next day that you are going to look forward to.

LORETTA: Yes!

THOM: Now, I'm guessing, Loretta, that there are things in your day that you don't like; that there are people in your world you don't like, that there are unpleasant things that happen from time to time.

LORETTA: I keep away from people like that, and there's really not too many, and if there is, I let them know it.

THOM: Well see, there you go. So my point is, though, that what you're choosing to focus on, because we all have negative things in our lives and we all have positive things in our lives. And Loretta, what you're choosing to focus on are the positives.

LORETTA: Right, that's correct.

THOM: And Pete, I would suggest to you that you might want to consider adopting Loretta's strategy. [talking to listeners] Now with Pete, here's a person whose primary motivational strategy is moving away from pain; it's become a habit, so his first instinct will probably be to try to change his strategy by creating a moving-away-from-pain strategy to do it. [talking to Pete] In other words, Pete, you would say, "Oh, well, I've got to stop thinking about negative things that might happen and so I'm going to figure out a way to punish myself if I think about them." And what I'm suggesting is a radical change. Instead of doing that, just allow yourself to think about the possibility that you have the resource for doing this moving-toward strategy. Pete, you've done it before many times in your life, I'm sure, of knowing that there is something out there that has a positive future that you want and you're looking forward to.

PETE: Sure.

THOM: And transfer that feeling of "Gee, I'm looking forward to that" to just creating a list before you go to sleep and reviewing it when you wake up, thinking of cool stuff that might happen during the day.

PFTF: Hey, that's a really good idea.

THOM: Okay. Try it out, and give us a call later in the week, Pete, and let us know how it worked, okay?

Pete called the show a few weeks later and said that he no longer needed an alarm clock to wake up in the mornings. The shift in strategies worked.

CREATING A "WE THE PEOPLE" CODE

To talk about Social Security, unemployment insurance, national health care, and other popular government programs, it's most useful to return to what is meaningful to voters about these programs. At their core, they contain both moving-toward-pleasure and moving-away-from-pain components.

Benefits most often speak directly to moving toward pleasure or away from pain, whereas *features,* being just data, rarely code either pain or pleasure.

Thus, instead of talking about just the *features* of these programs, like how much they cost per year and how many people they serve and so forth, it's important to start talking about their *benefits.* Answer the question: *Why would the average voter care about these programs?* From the voter's point of view, we must answer the question: *What's in it for me?*

One of the most vocal conservatives, Grover Norquist, once said, "I don't want to abolish government. I simply want to reduce it to the size where I can drag it into the bathroom and drown it in the bathtub."[4]

In 2005 we found out what happens when you follow Grover Norquist's advice and wash government down the drain. When Hurricane Katrina hit, more than a thousand people drowned in the basin of New Orleans. Our nation failed in its response because for most of the past quarter-century, starting with Ronald Reagan, conservatives who don't believe in government have been systematically dismantling every aspect of our government except those parts they can use to punish us or spy on us. (Remember that the conservative worldview is that intrinsically evil humans need restraining.)

When government creates programs, the programs are created by and for We the People. No one individual or company creates those programs for us: we create them for ourselves. We the People want security in our old age. We want to be able to keep paying our mortgage when we are between jobs. We want national health care so sickness won't bankrupt us. They are programs that *we* create for *our* own benefit, using the instrument of a representative government.

CODING SOCIAL SECURITY INSURANCE

Conservatives particularly love to attack the Social Security Insurance program (they don't even use it's real original name, which would be too descriptive for them to delete, distort, and generalize parts of, because it's really the federal Old Age, Survivors, and Disability Insurance [OASDI] program). Because Social Security is a government-run program that doesn't fall into the category of restraining or punishing behavior (police and armies), conservatives have a fundamental belief that such a program is not the business of government and should be best left to the mythical "free market."

But just saying this honestly and out loud is political suicide, so instead conservatives describe Social Security Insurance as an "old-age retirement program."

That frame involves a deletion. One-third of people who receive Social Security Insurance are neither retired nor old. They are the disabled, the severely and chronically ill, children born with birth defects, widows, orphans, and so forth.

It's also a distortion. Social Security Insurance is about securing the health and the welfare of *all* of society; the conservatives' description distorts it into a program that benefits a retired few.

And it's a generalization. Conservatives have generalized a piece of the overall Social Security Insurance program (its old-age poverty insurance program) and made it stand in for the whole.

Through that process of deleting, distorting, and generalizing Social Security and framing it as an old-age retirement program, conservatives purposely put Social Security into the "nanny state" frame. In this mapping of the territory, Social Security becomes yet another program that big government imposes on you and me, taxing us, taking our money, and then telling us that government knows better than we do how we should save for our retirement.

Once we begin using a frame someone else has constructed, we're constrained by their deletions, distortions, and generalizations. We can't counter this kind of argument by staying inside of the other person's story. Democrats lose when they say something like "Social Security is the best kind of old-age retirement program" or "your money is safer when it's run through this government program" because doing so implicitly accepts the conservatives' frame. The way to respond is to take back control of the story by proposing a more powerful frame and a more compelling story.

A Liberal Social Security Insurance Story

I travel a lot, often to developing countries. When I go to such places, it's not uncommon to find twenty or thirty children waiting each morning outside each of the "Western" or more affluent hotels with outstretched hands, begging for food. These children are sometimes orphans but most often simply come from families so poor their parents can't feed them. They are left on their own, to live or die, based on what they can beg or steal each day.

We in America have made a choice that we will feed such children; we've also made the aesthetic choice that we don't want to live in a society organized with such a rigid wealth order that we daily confront the face of extreme poverty. We are a kindhearted people (as liberals believe that the basic needs of all humans should be met). We want to feed the orphans, care for the widows, make sure the old are comfortable and the sick cared for. To do that we have created an insurance program that protects all of us from the sudden chances of poverty, sickness, or the death of a spouse. This program is called Social Security Insurance.

My dear friend and fellow writer Michael Hutchison, a man my age who lives in Santa Fe, New Mexico, broke his neck while he was out running about a decade ago. He's now paralyzed from the neck down, and he lives on Social Security. The same could happen to any of us, and Michael (and everybody who knows him) is grateful that FDR started the program and made it available to all Americans.

Social Security is an insurance policy that protects us from the greatest disasters in life; and because some of those disasters are so big, it takes all of us together to make it work. That's why we do this with and for each other, using a process and an institution we call government.

FROM MOTIVATION TO VALUES

The progressive Social Security Insurance story is simple. It counters the conservatives' investment/nanny state frame by offering an insurance policy/We the People frame. It shows how the insurance policy will be available to all of us because no matter how well off a person may be, we never know when disaster may strike (as many middle-class and moderately wealthy people discovered when the Republican Great Depression struck in 1929).

Although insurance is usually sold by motivating us away from some threat (think of the life insurance salesman with his tales about the impoverished family a breadwinner will leave behind), the larger story of Social Security creating a more secure and thus happier society motivates us toward compassion, a program "that works for all of us."

Liberals believe that Americans are compassionate and socially connected, and they call on that compassion to suggest that Social Security Insurance offers us a way to promise safety and security to ourselves and others. The power of these frames comes in large part from their ability to chunk up and down between these larger values and the specifics of their maps.

CHAPTER 13

CHUNKING
THE CODE

Did you, too, O friend, suppose democracy was only for elections,
for politics, and for a party name? I say democracy is only
of use there that it may pass on and come to its flower and
fruit in manners, in the highest forms of interaction between
[people], and their beliefs—in religion, literature, colleges
and schools—democracy in all public and private life....

— WALT WHITMAN

Even many Americans who are stockholders in the oil, gas, and coal industries have figured out that fossil fuels are overheating our planet. And most of us would like to do something about it. Almost everyone in the country is onboard with this idea, except for a small group of conservatives who still believe that dominating the Earth is what's best for them today and who don't worry about the legacy we will leave our children.

The main problem liberals have faced in talking about global warming has been creating a persuasive argument about what we all can do right now. Everyone sees the big picture, but we haven't been able to figure out how to talk about the small picture.

For example, most of our houses are run on natural gas and electricity. The electricity comes from power plants that, by and large, burn fossil fuels. It would be better for the planet if that electricity could come from geothermal, wind, and solar power. Because the sun is free to all and shines most days, anyone who owns property can become a solar power provider. Many of us who are homeowners could generate enough electricity to meet our needs by installing solar panels on our roofs, given the current state of the art of the technology.

I've talked with my neighbors about going solar. That's an elegant solution with just one problem: solar panels are expensive. They are expensive to buy and difficult to install. You can make back the money you spend on solar panels in energy savings, but unless you have an awfully big house and live somewhere the sun shines for eight hours a day every day, it's going to take you a few years to make that money back.[1]

I live in Portland, Oregon, and here in the Pacific Northwest, we have a long rainy season ("winter"), with day after day when the sun doesn't shine. Luckily, I like rain and fog, but all that wet weather means it'll take me longer to pay off an investment in solar technology than it will somebody who lives in Phoenix.

The solar panel argument works on the level of what I will call *the biggest chunk*—saving the planet—but it doesn't always work on the level of *the smallest chunk*—personal self-interest. Something might be very good for everyone but not work as well at the chunk of the individual.

CHUNKING

An argument can be made on any number of different levels, or *chunks*. In this example the smallest chunk is personal self-interest and the largest chunk is what's best for the planet. In between are chunks that include what's best for family, neighborhood, town, state, country, and so forth.

Each chunk is a map of a territory. Each chunk has its own story.

Abraham Lincoln, one of America's most competent communicators, used chunking with a healthy ecology in the Emancipation Proclamation. In that proclamation Lincoln suggested that ending slavery would be better for the individual congressman

LINCOLN'S EMANCIPATION PROCLAMATION

This is the segment of Lincoln's speech on the Emancipation Proclamation that shows how well Honest Abe chunked up and down to persuade his audience.

Is it doubted, then, that the plan I propose, if adopted, would shorten the war, and thus lessen its expenditure of money and of blood? Is it doubted that it would restore the national authority and national prosperity, and perpetuate both indefinitely? Is it doubted that we here—Congress and Executive— can secure its adoption? [all small chunks]

Will not the good people respond to a united, and earnest appeal from us? Can we, can they, by any other means, so certainly, or so speedily, assure these vital objects? We can succeed only by concert. [now the larger chunks]

It is not "can any of us imagine better?" but, "can we all do better?"

The dogmas of the quiet past, are inadequate to the stormy present. The occasion is piled high with difficulty, and we must rise—with the occasion. As our case is new, so we must think anew, and act anew.

We must disenthrall ourselves, and then we shall save our country.

Fellow-citizens, we cannot escape history. We of this Congress and this administration will be remembered in spite of ourselves. No personal significance, or insignificance, can spare one or another of us. The fiery trial through which we pass, will light us down, in honor or dishonor, to the latest generation.

We say we are for the Union. The world will not forget that we say this.

We know how to save the Union. The world knows we do know how to save it. We—even we here—hold the power, and bear the responsibility.

[now touching a small chunk and moving back to the largest chunk] In giving freedom to the slave, we assure

freedom to the free—honorable alike in what we give, and
what we preserve. We shall nobly save, or meanly lose, the last
best hope of earth. Other means may succeed; this could not
fail. The way is plain, peaceful, generous, just—a way which,
if followed, the world will forever applaud, and God must
forever bless. [You can also notice the modalities and future
pacing in this speech.]

(those who vote with him will receive "honor...to the latest generation"), better for the soldiers because it would bring a sooner
end to the Civil War (it "would shorten the war, and thus lessen its
expenditure of money and of blood"), and better for our values as
We the People ("In giving freedom to the slave, we assure freedom
to the free").

Lincoln framed the slavery issue in its smallest chunk (its
negative practical and moral impact on individuals) in virtually
the same breath as its largest chunk (ensuring the survival of the
nation). The small chunks are essential for people to understand
the *how* of something, but the big chunks provide the *why*. The
big chunks provide the *What is it?* while the small chunks usually
answer *What's in it for me?*

This is a variation on the features and the benefits mentioned
earlier. The features chunk explains what it is. The benefits chunk
answers the question *What's in it for me?* Features without benefits
have no relevance. Benefits without features have no credibility.
Together they are powerfully persuasive.

Lincoln was able to appeal to so many different interests without sounding scattered because he was ecological in his approach.
Each of the very different chunks he communicated was part of a
single ecological whole: what is better for members of his audience
and an individual congressman will also be better for the soldiers
and the war, will be better for the continuation of the Union, will
be better for We the People, and will be better for history. Details

and meaning. Features and benefits. Past and future. Big chunks and small. One and All.

CHUNKING SOLAR POWER

In the solar panel argument, there was a benefit at the largest chunk—saving the planet—and there were features to back up that benefit—solar panels use energy from the sun to create electricity, so homeowners don't need to use fossil fuels. We also know that solar panels can be used by almost any homeowner and that the energy source—the sun—is free. Those are both positive features that relate to the smallest chunk, the homeowner.

We also learned, however, that solar panels are expensive to purchase and install—so expensive, in fact, that many homeowners can't easily amortize the cost. At that chunk the solar panel argument is often not economically ecological because the benefits to the smallest chunk—the homeowner—and the largest chunk—the planet—don't match.

To make the argument work, create a benefit for the smallest chunk: if I can afford a solar panel for my house, and if I know that everyone in my community can afford a solar panel for their house, that is ecologically viable from the chunk of "me" all the way up to the chunk of planet Earth.

As it turns out, to create this benefit requires new features. That is exactly the logic that Germany used to pass the most progressive environmental legislation in the world.

In 1999 progressives in Germany passed the 100,000 Roofs Programme,[2] which mandated that banks had to provide low-interest ten-year loans to homeowners sufficient enough for them to put solar panels on their houses. They then passed the Renewable Energies Law in 2000,[3] which mandated that for the next ten years the power company had to buy back power from those homeowners at seven times the going rate, which would mean that the homeowners' income from the solar panels would equal their loan payments on the panels and would also represent the actual cost to the power company if, instead of people installing solar panels, they had decided to build a nuclear power plant.

Homeowners in Germany now can afford solar panels because the banks are giving them low-interest loans and the power companies are paying for the solar power generated by those panels at such a high rate that it equals the loan payments. It's like getting solar power panels for free. That's a benefit at the level of the homeowner chunk.

The power company is paying extra for power, but it had otherwise been planning to build a nuclear reactor to supply extra power. The cost to the power company of paying an unusually high rate for the energy generated by homeowners' solar panels is actually equal, over ten years, to the cost of building a new power plant. At the end of the ten years, the power company gets to buy solar power at its regular low rate, and it now has a new source of power without having to pay to maintain a nuclear reactor. That's a benefit at the largest chunk: the power company and society.

Germany provides the power its people need through passive solar panels rather than with a nuclear reactor. It also boosts its economy by providing customers for its burgeoning solar panel manufacturers, now some of the biggest in the world.[4] Germany becomes known as a leader in renewable resource technology, bringing additional companies and their taxes to the country. That's a benefit to the nation, and it moves everybody toward pleasure and away from pain.

Applying the Chunking Code

Once you have mastered chunking up and down the spectrum on one issue, you can apply the technique to many issues. Health care, for example, is an issue that remains a pressing concern for Americans.

Conservatives want health care to be even more privatized than it is now, with health-care vouchers replacing Medicare and Medicaid. They focus on the smallest chunk and suggest that we should focus on the importance of being able to choose our own doctor. I do want to choose my own doctor, but if I can't afford health insurance, I won't be able to choose any doctor, no matter what plans are out there. That's a midsized chunk.

Conservatives focus on the smallest chunk because their primary personal and internal motivation is fear, so they use fear of loss of choice to motivate people. Often the conservatives' arguments are not socially ecological, but few people notice because they stop at the first chunk, once their own personal fears and needs are addressed by the noble for-profit health insurance company that lets you choose among a few doctors.

The solution for liberals is to demonstrate how unecological the conservatives' arguments are by chunking up. Though conservatives like to say they are the party of "family values," their arguments usually focus only on the smallest chunk—individual rights—and rarely address the biggest chunk—true social values. Focusing on choosing one's doctor does not address our society's value that we all have the right to "life," which includes the right to get treatment if we are sick. Americans care deeply about that value.

The liberal argument for single-payer health insurance is ecological. With single-payer national (or at least state-by-state) health insurance, we benefit at the smallest chunk because we're guaranteed insurance; and, if the program has the same features as Medicare does, we would also benefit by getting to choose our own doctors. We also benefit at the biggest chunk because national heath insurance supports our values by guaranteeing that we all have the right to "life."

Once we understand that the map is not the territory, and that chunking is one way to define a message, mapping identity becomes a useful tool to control how the message is received.

CHAPTER 14

THE IDENTITY
CODE

*Feelings of worth can flourish only in an atmosphere where
individual differences are appreciated, mistakes are tolerated,
communication is open, and rules are flexible—the kind
of atmosphere that is found in a nurturing family.*

— VIRGINIA SATIR

When we communicate, there is a story, a storyteller, and a listener. The story travels from teller to listener, from writer to reader. Without people telling and listening, writing and reading, there would be no communication.

We began this book by talking about the importance of story. In part II we talked about the different ways people interact with the world, the way some people are primarily visual, some primarily auditory, some primarily kinesthetic, and so forth. In part III we talked about the importance of recognizing that someone else might not have the same response we have to a story and what techniques we can use to try to match their response to ours. In all of these discussions, we assumed that the person who is reading, or listening to, or experiencing our story has just one identity. We talked about ways people are different from each other, but we haven't yet talked about the different identities we each carry around inside ourselves.

Every day, we live out many different stories about ourselves. Another way of saying this is that we take on multiple identities to accomplish what we set out to do in the world. I am a husband to my wife, a father to my kids, a child to my mother, a friend to my friends, a boss to my employees, a performer to my radio listeners, an author to you, and so forth.

Many of us have experienced a personal "aha" moment when we saw or heard or felt who we *really* are, a deep and profound sense of personal identity and connection with all creation. Psychologists call that the *core self,* and Connirae and Tamara Andreas wrote a brilliant book about it in a therapeutic context, *Core Transformation: Reaching the Wellspring Within.* I learned much of what I know about this concept from a training session I took with them a decade ago (although the way I'm expressing this all is entirely mine—their expressions are much more elegant, detailed, and specific to therapy and personal growth and transformation).

Those moments when we discover our core selves are memorable because they don't come that often. Most of the time, we're inhabiting one of our many subidentities.

Each of these identities requires a different skill set. This doesn't mean that we're acting or playing a role or putting on a mask when we inhabit one of these identities. For example, the part of me you meet when I sign books is really me—but it's just one part of me. You probably won't meet the part of me who is a dad because it's not useful for me to be my dad part when I'm signing books.

There's that word *useful* again. By now you may have recognized that "usefulness" is a like a secret handshake for competent communicators. When you are an unconsciously competent communicator, you instinctively recognize which part of yourself is most useful when communicating with someone else. And you understand how to identify the part of the listener that will be most likely to connect with or listen to you.

Effective communication happens when your message matches the part of you that most cares about and most uses that message—and reaches the part of your listener that most cares about and uses that message. This is a form of map and territory congruence.

If you've been reading this book in a linear way, you may think you've read this before. *Matching your message to the person listening* may sound an awful lot like the theme of part III of this book, "The Meaning of a Communication Is the Response You Get." It is. The message of that section was that each of us is different from one another, so what persuades me may not be very persuasive to you. We talked about tools we can use—such as anchoring, future pacing, and the learning trance—to make it easier to persuade someone to at least pay attention when we communicate with him or her.

Mapping identity is also about your relationship with the person listening to you, but it goes even deeper. At this level of the communication code, we learn that even if you are talking to just one person, there is not just one "me" talking and not just one "me" listening. Each of us has multiple identities, and what is persuasive to one part of me may not be persuasive to another part of me. To increase the effectiveness of the techniques in part III, we need to map out our listener's identity and figure out which part will be most effective to speak with.

CREATING MINI-ME'S

In the 1999 Mike Myers's movie *The Spy Who Shagged Me,* the hero Austin Powers has a little problem with his nemesis, Dr. Evil. Dr. Evil has cloned a part of himself and named the one-eighth-sized clone Mini-Me. Dr. Evil created Mini-Me because he felt he wasn't quite evil enough; he created Mini-Me out of his frighteningly curled pinky finger—his purely evil part. Mini-Me can't talk—or at least can't talk much—because an evil part doesn't really need to talk. He writes notes and fights (unfairly) very well. Whenever Dr. Evil seems to be in danger of showing the least bit of compassion or humanity, Mini-Me scribbles him a note to buck up his evil side. He's a very useful sidekick to have around for a fictional character like Dr. Evil.

Mini-Me gets most of the laughs in the film. It's funny to see a pint-size version of an already cartoonish character, and actor Verne Troyer does a great job of imitating actor Mike Myers's Dr. Evil. As with most jokes, though, there's also a germ of truth. All of us create Mini-Me's, parts of ourselves that take on a life and an identity of their own. We create them because, like Dr. Evil, we find them useful.

It's easiest to identify the different mini-me's that play defined social roles in the world, such as my dad part, my friend part, and so on. These are identities that are created by our relationships with other people. Closer to our core, we have identities that we create from our own needs and desires. For example, I have a curious part, a hungry part, a compassionate part, a spiritual part, and so on. Being human, I also have a selfish part, a vengeful part, and a part capable of expressing anger. We create parts for every aspect of our being.

These parts have developed because they are useful to us. When we are born, parts emerge to accomplish certain tasks and to meet specific needs. Crying was a behavior controlled by one of our first parts, a part we developed because we needed a way to tell the world that we were hungry. Every time a new need arose, a new part of our brain was activated as a resource to meet that need. One part took responsibility for getting the diapers changed, another for getting fed, another for getting affection, and so forth.

As we go through life, we develop a whole repertory of parts. An entire cast of these parts develops to handle particular desires, needs, problems, and crises. Very often these parts were momentary loci of focused energy and attention; and when they were finished with their job, they dissolved back into your core self, the totality that is you. Others were created to meet ongoing and life-long needs, such as the need to be fed, or the need for attention, or the need to protect the body. These parts tend to come into being when we face large life changes, such as going to kindergarten, engaging in our first romantic relationship, leaving home, suffering a deep personal loss, and so on.

The parts that emerge to provide us with important new skill sets can take on relatively independent lives of their own. They each have a unique identity and personality. That's why it's more useful to say that there are multiple "me's" than to talk about just one "me."

"Wait," you might say. "You make it sound like each of us has multiple-personality disorder." We do each have multiple personalities, but for most of us they are not disordered. Most mental health issues grow out of structures already present in the brain. The difference between someone who is mentally healthy and someone who has multiple-personality disorder (MPD) is that with MPD one part takes over, gives itself a name, and causes amnesia about all the other parts. In a mentally healthy person, a part takes center stage when needed but is aware of the other parts and, in fact, interacts with them.

For example, I can use my teaching part while I write this section of this book, and at the same time I'm drawing on my friend part (thinking of you in a positive way, trying to give you something useful) and my parent part (hoping to equip you for the world, to one day see you fly on your own). Mentally healthy people unconsciously and intuitively understand that each of these parts is "me" and that collectively they make up the larger "me."

We juggle our different parts all the time. The part that comes to the fore when you are having a fight is very different from the part in charge when you are falling in love; and both are quite different from the part that takes charge when you are applying for a job, dealing with a store clerk, or advocating for something you believe in.

Therapists can use this information about our different parts to heal dysfunctional parts and help us find our core self. I talk about how to do that in my book *Healing ADD*.[1] When we communicate specific, individual-issue messages, however, we almost always want to speak to a particular part. Consider how George W. Bush spoke to our hurt and vengeful parts when he used the bullhorn at Ground Zero in New York. Or how some politicians speak to their constituents' fearful child parts when they repeatedly invoke 9/11 "be afraid" frames. That's because each part has its own function, and we can use the differences between parts to control how our message is heard. This is the key to cracking the *identity code.*

THE NASCAR DAD

What makes the identity code so powerful is that it also allows us to chunk up to communicate with many people at the same time. A real communication expert can put a whole group of people into a learning trance or throw them into the future.

The Republican Party, for example, recently targeted the so-called "NASCAR dad." The NASCAR dad does not define a group of people but rather *an identity* that is shared by a large group of people.

Many different kinds of people like to watch car racing.[2] More than 75 million people enjoy watching this sport. And 40 percent—almost half of these fans—are women. Forty-two percent—almost half—earn more than $50,000 per year. And only 38 percent of these NASCAR fans come from the South, matching exactly the spread of the U.S. population (35 percent of the U.S. population lives in the South). So the average NASCAR fan could just as easily be a well-to-do woman from the mountain states as a working-class guy from the South.

The term *NASCAR dad* doesn't describe these people's age or wealth or geographic status—or even their gender. It describes a part, which is uniquely identifiable and touches a larger sense of identity. Men and women (and kids) who watch NASCAR—like nearly all Americans—like to think of themselves as patriots. When they watch the car races and share that experience with others similarly enthusiastic about it, they experience themselves as "regular," "genuine," "down to earth" kinds of people.[3] It is *this* identity, the "ordinary patriotic American" part, that Republicans wanted to target to cause the NASCAR psychographic to delete from consciousness the wealthy corporate elite who are the true Republican base.

TARGETING THE FEAR PART'S CODE

George W. Bush usually focused his message on just a few parts—and made sure his message was congruent to those parts. The parts Bush spoke to are mostly our vengeful and fearful parts (presumably because those are the most prominent/powerful parts within him).

We all have parts that are responsible for safety and security. Those are basic needs. In most people those parts are preverbal, instinctual, and very powerful. They are powerful enough to override the intellect parts because they're in charge of survival. When Republicans crafted messages directly to those parts, they had tremendous power.

Almost every speech Bush gave was set up to appeal, in large or small ways, to our fearful parts, the parts responsible for safety and security. In March 2007, for example, Bush gave a speech to cattle ranchers, one of his favorite groups. Most vote Republican and come from Texas, Bush's adopted home state. The main part of the speech was about the economy. Bush trotted out the frames his handlers had given him: he talked about the "death tax" and about his belief that "only you know best what to do with 'your money.'"

These frames could be used to appeal to many different parts. They could appeal to the cattlemen's selfish parts, or they could appeal to their self-righteous parts. But Bush found a way to make these economic frames appeal to their fearful part. Notice, along the way, that he also used the "indirect you" code (see chapter 6). He said:

> You know, when you cut the individual tax rates, you affect farmers and ranchers. Many farmers and ranchers are Sub-chapter S corporations, or limited partnerships, or sole proprietorships, which means you pay tax at the individual income tax level. And if you're worried about a vibrant agricultural economy, it makes sense to let those who work the land keep more of their own money so they can invest, so they can make the necessary changes so that their businesses can remain vibrant.

This is a pretty interesting way to sell tax cuts. Bush uses the word "invest," but he's not really telling these ranchers that tax cuts will make their businesses bigger or better. He's suggesting that they have something to "worry" about and that they need these tax cuts just "so that their businesses can remain vibrant." No tax cuts, Mr. Rancher, and your business is gonna collapse faster than a rickety fence in a tornado. It's an implied threat. Bush is telling these good old boys that if they don't get their tax cuts, their businesses aren't going to survive. They won't "remain vibrant." They will lose out in the global free trade wars (which his father helped create in the first place).

This speech is a classic example of motivating listeners away from pain. Each of us has parts that protect us from threats. If you tell us something painful or scary might happen and give us a way to avoid it, we are pretty likely to do as told, as those parts are very powerful.

Bush used the same strategy, in the same speech, in an even clearer way when he shifts to talking about the war in Iraq. In March 2007 things weren't looking too good for Bush's war. The

House and the Senate had both voted on bills setting a deadline for withdrawal. Polls showed that Americans were not pleased with the war and wanted to bring the troops home. So there was Bush, standing before a very friendly audience, wanting to rehearse his most powerful argument in favor of staying the course:

> September the 11th is an important moment in this country's history. It's a sad moment. But it should serve as a wake-up call to the realities of the world in which we live. On September the 11th, we saw problems originating in a failed state some 7,000 miles away that affected how we live. See, September the 11th was not only a day we were attacked, it is a day that our country must never forget, and the lessons of that day must never be forgot, that what happens overseas matters here at home. It may be tempting to say, oh, just let it run its natural course. But for me, allowing the world to run its natural course, which could lead to more violence and hatred, would end up reducing the security of the United States, not enhancing the security. And our biggest job in America, the biggest job of this government, is to protect you from harm.

Bush always likes to start any discussion of war with 9/11 because 9/11 has become an anchor for every American tied directly to our most fearful and our most protective parts. When we even hear or see the numbers "9/11" many of us immediately bring forward our protective parts. By 2007 even the pro-war cattle ranchers listening to this speech probably were aware that Iraq and 9/11 were completely unrelated.

Bush starts his discussion of the Iraq war with 9/11 anyway, however, because no matter what the price may be in terms of conscious pushback or even derision, he wants to go directly to his listeners' unconscious but incredibly powerful fearful and protective parts. Using the "you" code again, Bush builds up these parts until he gets to his punch line: the ranchers should support him in any kind of war because Bush will "protect you from harm." That's just what the fearful part, once it's evoked, needs to hear.[4]

George W. Bush can be stumblingly inarticulate. But author and New York University professor Mark Crispin Miller writes in *The Bush Dyslexicon* that, "Bush is almost always clear when he's speaking cruelly. For example, when the subject is punitive infliction of great pain, there is no problem with his syntax, grammar, or vocabulary, even if he happens to be lying.... Like all the rest of us, however well or badly educated, Bush can talk quite clearly on the subjects that most interest him: baseball, football, campaign tactics, putting men to death."[5]

On the other hand, Miller notes that "when he tries to feign idealism or compassion, the man stops speaking his own native language." Bush speaks very clearly when he is speaking from his vengeful part, his angry part, and his tough-guy part. He knows how to address the vengeful, angry, and fearful parts in us as well. He's not so good at speaking from his compassionate part or his understanding part as these are apparently stunted or well muffled by some protective part within him.

Targeting Our Best Parts

The vengeful, angry, fearful, and protective parts of us are very powerful. Conservative message-makers love those parts because when people are looking for revenge or protection all the time, they're more likely to embrace authority figures. I talk about that in my book *Screwed*. But there is an alternative.

Martin Luther King Jr., Gandhi, and Jesus talked to our compassionate parts, our hopeful parts, our idealistic parts. King moved a nation when he told us he had a dream. Gandhi transformed continents when he advocated nonviolence. Jesus changed the course of the world when he told us that the meaning of life is love. Although at any given hour or day, the fearful part can seem the stronger part, these examples down through the ages remind us that hope is ultimately stronger than fear and that love is stronger than hate.

Republicans under the Bush administration have focused virtually all of their messages around fear: "Look out! Saddam's going to get you." "Look out! Iran is going to get you." If you are not afraid enough about what's happening abroad, they will scare you right at home: "Look out! Social Security is in crisis!" "Look out! The government wants to take your money!" Republicans consistently appeal to the vengeful, frightened, protective parts of us all.

Liberals generally appeal more often to our natural allies—the hopeful, idealistic, and compassionate parts we all share. Presidents like John F. Kennedy and Franklin D. Roosevelt spoke to our hopeful parts. Here's Kennedy, speaking during the fourth debate he had with Richard Nixon:[6]

> I believe that if we can get a party which believes in movement, which believes in going ahead, then we can reestablish our position in the world, strong in defense, strong in economic growth, justice for our people, co-guarantee of constitutional rights, so that people will believe that we practice what we preach.

To move forward, to hold a positive vision—that is a powerful message we can use to appeal to our collective, societal hopeful part. Imagine how our country would change for the better if politicians today followed in the footsteps of JFK and FDR and really told the liberal story.

RECLAIMING THE LIBERAL STORY

Liberalism is trust of the people, tempered by prudence;
conservatism, distrust of people, tempered by fear.

— WILLIAM GLADSTONE

The communication code is the internal structure we all use to translate language and image and experience into meaning, to convert territories into useful maps.

We express our identities in every aspect of our communication, from the modalities we use to the frames we create. When we communicate, we're saying something about who we are—in each of our parts, as whole individuals, and as members of our society.

When you chunk all the way up, you find that every communication is part of a larger story about who We the People are. Each little story we tell ourselves is also a story about liberty, about democracy, about community. They are stories about what it means to be a citizen of the United States and what it means to be a citizen of the world. They are, ultimately, stories about what it means to be human.

What we call politics is no more and no less than that collection of stories.

THE REPUBLICANS' STORY

When Democratic strategists try to understand the people who voted for Ronald Reagan and George W. Bush, they assume that those voters were making decisions based on issues like abortion, free trade, taxes, and so forth. They think that when Joan Smith says, "I am a Republican," she agrees with all the positions that Republicans take on a laundry list of issues.

In fact, if you poll the John and Joan Smiths who identify themselves as Republicans, you will find that many of them disagree with almost all of the planks of the official Republican Party platform and would aggressively agree with most of the parts of the Democratic Party's agenda.

The Republican Party is on record in favor of overturning *Roe v. Wade,* but 62 percent of the American people want the *Roe v. Wade* ruling to stand.[1] The Republican Party is on record as believing that taxes should be lowered, but in 2006 a full 60 percent of Americans said that the amount of income tax they paid that year was fair.[2] The Republican Party has denied or downplayed global warming, but 60 percent of Americans think that global warming is already happening, and 70 to 80 percent are worried about pollution of our air and water.[3] Finally, it was the Republican Party that gave us the Iraq war, but as the 2008 elections approached, 70 percent of Americans disapproved of that war and 60 percent wanted the United States to get out.[4]

Joan Smith, it turns out, doesn't actually care that much about the Republican platform. What she cares about is the *story* that goes along with the word *Republican.*

Being a Republican is a multimodal experience that evokes a very particular feeling. The visual modality (brand/logo) they have claimed is the American flag. The auditory modality is "Stars and Stripes Forever." The kinesthetic modality they've imprinted on their followers is "standing tough, standing tall, and pulling yourself up by your bootstraps." These modalities anchor a feeling of security, which reinforces the conservative core story that the world is a bad place and that we need a few, rare, powerful, "good" paternalistic people to protect us from it.

In 2004 Andrew Card, then President Bush's chief of staff, explained to Republican delegates from Maine how Bush understood his role in the conservative story. Card said, "'It struck me as I was speaking to people in Bangor, Maine, that this president sees America as we think about a ten-year-old child.' Card added, "I know as a parent I would sacrifice all for my children."[5]

Anyone who believes the traditional American liberal story finds Card's suggestion that we should think of ourselves as children offensive. We are grown adults with rights and responsibilities and the inherent ability to make good decisions derived from our own intrinsic goodness. From the conservative point of view, however, Card's story was reassuring. Conservatives want to be protected from their own latent evil and the explicit evil of all other people, and the president was offering that protection.

This kind of example demonstrates that the conservative core story Republicans tell themselves is not just a metaphor. The conservative core story of fear and hierarchy actually defines and creates the modern Republican identity.

THE DEMOCRATS' STORY

The American flag, "Stars and Stripes Forever," and standing tall and tough were all solidly Democratic "brands" during the presidencies of FDR and JFK. When we think "Democrat" today, Americans often don't see a particular image, hear a particular sound, or feel a particular emotion. That's a real problem because the communication code is based on those modalities. It illustrates why it's so important for Democrats to reclaim the American flag and the national anthem as their logos and traditional, egalitarian American democracy as their brand.

Republicans talk a lot about the benefits of *their* brand and programs—their followers will feel safer, be more secure, and have control over "their" money. Conversely, Democrats often are mired in lengthy descriptions of *features.* Most Democrats know all the features they are interested in: universal single-payer health care, a viable social safety net, prison and sentencing reform, a livable wage, support for unions, and voting reforms, for example. But there's no explicit "benefit" statement in lists of features/programs like these.

Republicans have learned from their allies in big business the importance of branding and leading with benefits. They sold everyone on the benefits of lowering taxes so "you can keep more of your money" (without telling us that they were actually going to borrow "our" money from our children and grandchildren) *before* they rolled out tax cuts for the wealthy. They sold the benefit of living in a society that "protects children" *before* rolling out deceptive legislation and PR stunts equating homosexuality with pedophilia.

Democrats have forgotten that the meaning of a communication is the response you get. They've forgotten that to be persuasive, they must tailor their map to their audience's territory.

WE THE PEOPLE

The traditional American liberal story is the story of We the People.

As Americans, the most important part of our social identity is our role as citizens. To be a citizen means to be part of, and a defender of, the commons of our nation. The water we drink, the air we breathe, the streets we drive on, the schools that we use, the fire departments that protect us—these are all the physical commons. And there are also the cultural commons—the stories we tell ourselves, our histories, our religions, and our notions of ourselves. And there are the commons of our power systems (in the majority of American communities), our health-care system (stolen from us and privatized over the past twenty-five years, our hospitals in particular used to be mostly nonprofit or run by mostly city or county governments), and the electronic commons of our radio and TV spectrum and the Internet. Most important for citizenship is the commons of government—the creation and the servant of We the People.

Franklin D. Roosevelt understood this commons. In his "Four Freedoms" speech, he said, "Necessitous men are not free men." Hungry people aren't free people, no matter what you want to call them. Hungry people can't be good citizens: they're too busy taking care of the hungry part of themselves to care about the citizen part.

Republicans don't want to fund FDR's social safety net because they fundamentally do not believe in the concept of We the People collectively protecting all of *us* in anything other than a military/police way. They don't believe that "the rabble" should run the country. They want big corporations to run the commons of our nation, and they think that the most appropriate role for citizens is that of infantilized consumers—of both commercial products and commercially produced political packaging.

This is the fundamental debate in our society: Are we a nation of citizens or a nation of consumers? Are we a democracy run by citizens, or are we a corporatocracy that holds consumers locked in dependency by virtue of their consumption?

Consumerism appeals to the greedy and selfish child part of us, the infantilized part that just wants someone else to take care of us. The core message of most commercials is that "you are the most important person in the world." Commercial advertising almost never mentions "we" or "us."

What is at stake today is the very future of our democratic republic. If we accept an identity as fearful, infantilized consumers, we will be acting from our baby part and allowing corporate America and an increasingly authoritarian government to fill the role of a parent part.

The story we are told is that we should surrender all of our power to corporations and just let them govern us because a mystical but all-knowing godlike force called "the free market" will eventually solve all of our problems.

That story fits in very well with the conservatives' other story: that we are children who need to be protected from evil humans; and because corporations are amoral and not human, they are intrinsically and morally superior to evil humans.

To save democracy we must crack that code and bring back the code so well understood by the Founders of this nation: that we're a country of barn-builders, of communities, of intrinsically *good* people who work together for the common good and the common wealth. We begin this process by speaking to the responsible part of us, the part that enjoys being grown up and socially responsible.

The story we have to tell is the story of citizenship, derived from our best and most noble parts. It's the story of We the People.

We talk a lot about the features of citizenship, like the right to vote, but we sometimes forget what the benefits are. The main benefit of citizenship is freedom—not freedom from external or internal dangers (although that is included in the package, it's only *one* of the six purposes listed in the Preamble to the Constitution) that conservatives obsess on, but freedom to think as we want, to pray as we want, to say what we want, and to live as we want to fulfill our true potential as humans (the other *five* things listed in the Preamble).

The question, ultimately, is whether our nation will continue to stand for the values on which it was founded.

Early American conservatives suggested that democracy was so ultimately weak it couldn't withstand the assault of newspaper editors and citizens who spoke out against it, leading John Adams (our second president and our first conservative president) to pass America's first Military Commissions Act–like laws: the Alien and Sedition Acts of 1798. President Thomas Jefferson, who beat Adams in the "Revolution of 1800" election, rebuked those who wanted America ruled by an iron-handed presidency that could—as Adams had—throw people in jail for "crimes" such as speaking political opinion, and without constitutional due process.

"I know, indeed," Jefferson said in his first inaugural address on March 4, 1801, "that some honest men fear that a republican government cannot be strong; that this government is not strong enough." But, Jefferson said, our nation was "the world's best hope" precisely because we put our trust in We the People.

Who Will Tell the Traditional American Liberal Story?

When I was working in Russia some years ago, a friend in Kaliningrad told me a perhaps apocryphal story about Nikita Khrushchev, who, following Stalin's death, gave a speech to the Politburo denouncing Stalin's policies of arbitrarily arresting people and throwing them in prisons or mental institutions without rights of habeas corpus. A few minutes into Khrushchev's diatribe, somebody in the back of the Politburo audience shouted out, "Why didn't you denounce Stalin then, the way you are now?"

The room fell silent, as Khrushchev swept the audience with his glare. "Who said that?" he asked in a reasoned voice. Silence.

"Who said that?" Khrushchev demanded, leaning forward, his voice tinged with anger. Silence.

Pounding his fist on the podium to accent each word, he screamed, "Who—said—that?!" Still no answer.

Finally, after a long and strained silence, the elected politicians in the room afraid to even cough, a corner of Khrushchev's mouth lifted into a smile.

"Now you know," he said with a chuckle, "why I did not speak up against Stalin when I sat where you now sit."

The question for our day is *Who will speak up against authoritarian policies in America?* Who will speak against politicians who abuse American democracy by punishing reporters and news

organizations through cutting off their access, who punish politicians by targeting them in their home districts, who punish truth-
tellers in the Executive branch by character assassination that even
extends to destroying their spouses' careers?

We must not make the mistake that Jefferson warned us
against. We must not remain silent, like Khrushchev's people did.
We must speak out.

We are citizens. It's time to reclaim that identity. And with
the tools of competent communicators, each of us is equipped to
tell the story of We the People and restore our democracy.

Democracy begins with you. Tag—you're it!

NOTES

CHAPTER 1

CRACKING THE WORLDVIEW CODE

1. Thomas Frank, "Coal Mine Deaths Spiked Upward," *USA Today,* January 1, 2007; http://www.usatoday.com/news/nation/2007-01-01-mine_x .htm. Also see Mike Hall, "Last Year's Coal Mine Deaths Increase 210 Percent Over 2005," July 20, 2006; http://blog.aflcio.org/2006/07/20/ sago-mine-deaths-could-have-been-prevented.

2. Here's just one grim example of the cuts in funding for music education from a San Diego paper: Chris Moran, "Low Note Sounds for Music Education," November 19, 2004; http://www.signonsandiego.com/union trib/20041119/news_7m19music.html.

3. See http://www.richardbandler.com. For a first introduction to these ideas, I suggest reading Richard Bandler and John Grinder, *Frogs into Princes: Neuro-Linguistic Programming* (Boulder: Real People Press, 1979).

4. Thomas Hobbes's *Leviathan,* which outlined his philosophy that human beings are fundamentally selfish, was published in 1651. John Locke's *Two Treatises on Government,* which influenced the Declaration of Independence, was published in 1690.

5. From *Leviathan;* http://www.literature.org/authors/hobbes-thomas/ leviathan. Hobbes wrote:

   To describe the nature of this artificial man, I will consider
   - First, the matter thereof, and the artificer; both which is man.
   - Secondly, how, and by what covenants it is made; what are the rights and just power or authority of a sovereign; and what it is that preserveth and dissolveth it.
   - Thirdly, what is a Christian Commonwealth.
   - Lastly, what is the Kingdom of Darkness.

6. Ibid. Hobbes wrote:

   Nature hath made men so equall, in the faculties of body, and mind; as that though there bee found one man sometimes manifestly stronger in body, or of quicker mind then another; yet when all is reckoned together, the difference between man, and man, is not so considerable, as that one man can thereupon claim to himselfe any benefit, to which another may not pretend, as well as he. For as to the strength of body, the weakest has strength enough to kill the strongest, either by secret machination, or by confederacy with others, that are in the same danger with himselfe.

And as to the faculties of the mind, (setting aside the arts grounded upon words, and especially that skill of proceeding upon generall, and infallible rules, called Science; which very few have, and but in few things; as being not a native faculty, born with us; nor attained, (as Prudence,) while we look after somewhat els,) I find yet a greater equality amongst men, than that of strength. For Prudence, is but Experience; which equall time, equally bestowes on all men, in those things they equally apply themselves unto. That which may perhaps make such equality incredible, is but a vain conceipt of ones owne wisdome, which almost all men think they have in a greater degree, than the Vulgar; that is, than all men but themselves, and a few others, whom by Fame, or for concurring with themselves, they approve. For such is the nature of men, that howsoever they may acknowledge many others to be more witty, or more eloquent, or more learned; Yet they will hardly believe there be many so wise as themselves: For they see their own wit at hand, and other mens at a distance. But this proveth rather that men are in that point equall, than unequall. For there is not ordinarily a greater signe of the equall distribution of any thing, than that every man is contented with his share.

7. Hobbes wrote the following paragraphs under the heading "Of The Naturall Condition Of Mankind, As Concerning Their Felicity, And Misery":

From this equality of ability, ariseth equality of hope in the attaining of our Ends. And therefore if any two men desire the same thing, which neverthelesse they cannot both enjoy, they become enemies; and in the way to their End, (which is principally their owne conservation, and sometimes their delectation only,) endeavour to destroy, or subdue one an other.

8. Ibid. Hobbes wrote:

And from this diffidence of one another, there is no way for any man to secure himselfe, so reasonable, as Anticipation; that is, by force, or wiles, to master the persons of all men he can, so long, till he see no other power great enough to endanger him: And this is no more than his own conservation requireth, and is generally allowed. Also because there be some, that taking pleasure in contemplating their own power in the acts of conquest, which they pursue farther than their security requires; if others, that otherwise would be glad to be at ease within modest bounds, should not by invasion increase their power, they would not be able, long time, by standing only on their defence, to subsist. And by consequence, such augmentation of dominion over men, being necessary to a mans conservation, it ought to be allowed him.

Againe, men have no pleasure, (but on the contrary a great deale of griefe) in keeping company, where there is no power able to over-awe them all.

9. Ibid. Hobbes wrote:

Out Of Civil States, There Is Alwayes Warre
Of Every One Against Every One

Hereby it is manifest, that during the time men live without a common Power to keep them all in awe, they are in that condition which is called Warre; and such a warre, as is of every man, against every man. For WARRE, consisteth not in Battell onely, or the act of fighting; but in a tract of time, wherein the Will to contend by Battell is sufficiently known: and therefore the notion of Time, is to be considered in the nature of Warre; as it is in the nature of Weather. For as the nature of Foule weather, lyeth not in a showre or two of rain; but in an inclination thereto of many dayes together: So the nature of War, consisteth not in actuall fighting; but in the known disposition thereto, during all the time there is no assurance to the contrary. All other time is PEACE.

10. Ibid. Hobbes wrote:

For the savage people in many places of America, except the government of small Families, the concord whereof dependeth on naturall lust, have no government at all; and live at this day in that brutish manner, as I said before. Howsoever, it may be perceived what manner of life there would be, where there were no common Power to feare; by the manner of life, which men that have formerly lived under a peacefull government, use to degenerate into, in a civill Warre.

11. For an overview of Riane Eisler's thought and that of others on dominator culture, see http://www.partnershipway.org.

12. John Locke, in Two Treatises on Government:

> First, It is not, nor can possibly be absolutely arbitrary over the lives and fortunes of the people: for it being but the joint power of every member of the society given up to that person, or assembly, which is legislator; it can be no more than those persons had in a state of nature before they entered into society, and gave up to the community: for no body can transfer to another more power than he has in himself; and no body has an absolute arbitrary power over himself, or over any other, to destroy his own life, or take away the life or property of another.
>
> A man, as has been proved, cannot subject himself to the arbitrary power of another; and having in the state of nature no arbitrary power over the life, liberty, or possession of another, but only so much as the law of nature gave him for the preservation of himself, and the rest of mankind; this is all he cloth, or can give up to the common-wealth, and by it to the legislative power, so that the legislative can have no more than this. Their power, in the utmost bounds of it, is limited to the public good of the society. It is a power, that hath no other end but preservation, and therefore can never have a right to destroy, enslave, or designedly to impoverish the subjects. The obligations of the law of nature cease not in society, but only in many cases are drawn closer, and have by human laws known penalties annexed to them, to inforce their observation. Thus the law of nature stands as an eternal rule to all men, legislators as well as others. The rules that they make for other men's actions, must, as well as their own and other men's actions, be conformable to the law of nature...

13. Thomas Jefferson, in *Autobiography* (1821):

> The next event which excited our sympathies for Massachusetts was the Boston port bill, by which that port was to be shut up on the 1st of June, 1774. This arrived while we were in session in the spring of that year.

14. In 2006 a Zogby poll showed that 46 percent still believed that Hussein helped plan the attacks (www.zogby.com; September 5, 2006). That number continues to drop as people become disillusioned with the Iraq war.

15. See "President Bush Outlines Iraqi Threat," http://www.whitehouse .gov/news/releases/2002/10/20021007-8.html.

CHAPTER 3

CRACKING THE SENSORY CODE

1. As cited in Association for Education in Journalism and Mass Communication conference paper by Elliott Parker, October 30, 2004; http://list.msu.edu/cgi-bin/wa?A2=ind0410e&L=aejmc&T=0&P=1472.

CHAPTER 4

THE BODY'S SECRET LANGUAGE

1. See Richard Bandler and John Grindler, *The Structure of Magic* vols. I and II (1975, 1976); *Patterns of the Hypnotic Techniques of Milton H. Erickson,* vols. I and II (1975, 1977); and Bandler, *Changing with Families: a Book About Further Education for Being Human* (1976).

2. See "Willie Horton: Is Dukakis Soft on Crime?" http://www.cnn.com/ALLPOLITICS/1996/candidates/ad.archive.

3. See "Candidate Ads: 1988 George Bush 'Revolving Door'"; http://www.insidepolitics.org/ps111/candidateads.html.

4. See "Mike Dukakis and the Massachusetts Miracle" campaign brochure at http://www.4president.org/brochures/dukakis1988brochure.htm.

5. See http://www.insidepolitics.org/ps111/candidateads.html.

6. A. Hennenlotter, U. Schroeder, P. Erhard, et al., "A Common Neural Basis for Receptive and Expressive Communication of Pleasant Facial Affect." *NeuroImage* (2005) 26(2): 581–91; http://www.ncbi.nlm.nih.gov/entrez.

7. R. B. Zajonc. "Emotion and Facial Efference: A Theory Reclaimed." *Science* (1985) 228(4695): 15–21.

8. R. B. Zajonc. "Feeling and Thinking: Preferences Need No Inferences." *American Psychologist* (1980) 35(2): 151–75.

CHAPTER 5

HOW FEELINGS ARE ANCHORED

1. See http://www.fair.org/index.php?page=1276.

2. Remarks of Senator Hillary Rodham Clinton on privacy to the American Constitution Society, June 16, 2006; http://www.senate.gov/~clinton/news/statements/details.cfm?id=257288.

CHAPTER 6

THE "NEGATIVE" CODE

1. Search "Michael Richards rant" at http://www.youtube.com.

2. See "Richards Says Anger, Not Racism, Sparked Tirade," November 2, 2006; http://www.msnbc.msn.com/id/15816126.

3. Sean C. Draine and Anthony G. Greenwald, "Unconscious Processing of Two-word Negations: A 'Not Bad' Experiment." Poster presented at the APS meeting in San Francisco, June 1996; http://www.millisecond.com/seandr/psych.

4. "Health Care Reform in the United States: Arguments for a Single Payer System," HRG Publication #1778, July 28, 2006; http://www.citizen.org/publications/release.cfm?ID=7446&secID=1158&catID=126.

5. NewsMax.com, February 20, 2007; http://www.newsmax.com/archives/ic/2007/2/20/100044.shtml?s=ic.

CHAPTER 7

THE CODE OF THE CORE STORY

1. Papers of Dwight David Eisenhower, Document #1147, November 8, 1954; http://www.eisenhowermemorial.org/presidential-papers/first-term/documents/1147.cfm.

2. Robert Ajemian, Michael Riley, and Michael Dukakis, "An Interview with Michael Dukakis," *Time,* November 7, 1988; http://www.time.com/time/magazine/article/0,9171,968844-2,00.html.

3. For example, in December 2006 in Kansas, outgoing Republican Attorney General Phil Kline filed 30 misdemeanor charges against abortion provider Dr. George Tiller. New Democratic Attorney General Paul Morrison dropped the charges.

4. Bernie Sanders, "U.S. Needs a Political Revolution," CommonDreams.org, August 17, 2001; http://www.commondreams.org/views01/0817-05.htm.

CHAPTER 8

MASTERING THE LEARNING TRANCE

1. The "World View" ad is available at the Stanford archive, http://pcl.stanford.edu/campaigns/campaign2004/archive.html.

CHAPTER 9

FUTURE PACING

1. Erin McCormick, "Anti-war activists take Pelosi to task: Minority leader negotiates with lawmakers to her right," SFGate.com, January 15, 2006; http://www.sfgate.com/cgi-bin/article.cgi?file=/c/a/2006/01/15/BAGSMGNJDL15.DTL.

2. Dan Balz, "Pelosi Hails Democrats' Diverse War Stances," Washington Post.com, December 16, 2005; http://www.washingtonpost.com/wp-dyn/content/article/2005/12/15/AR2005121501814.html.

3. Josephine Hearn and Mike Allen, "Pelosi Says She Wasn't Consulted on Iraq," CBSNews.com, January 25, 2007; http://www.cbsnews.com/stories/2007/01/25/politics/main2397489.shtml.

4. "Exclusive: Pelosi Says Bush 'Has to Answer for This War,'" ABCnews.com; http://abcnews.go.com/GMA/story?id=2805714&page=2.

5. Veterans front and center during Iraq debate," CNN.com, February 13, 2007; http://www.cnn.com/2007/POLITICS/02/13/us.iraq/index.html.

CHAPTER 10

FRAMING

1. To give conservatives their due, they try to make a case that gun ownership lowers crime. Yet all the statistics they can marshal are indirect and may have other causes. For a good example, see this paper defending gun ownership by the very highly regarded conservative think tank, the Cato Institute: David B. Kopel, "Trust the People: The Case Against Gun Control," July 11, 1988; http://www.cato.org/pubs/pas/pa109.html.

2. "Firearm Statistics," athealth.com; http://www.athealth.com/Consumer/issues/gunviolencestats.html.

3. "Canada–US Comparison," Coalition for Gun Control, http://www.guncontrol.ca/Content/Cda-US.htm.

4. "New Poll Finds Americans Support Estate Tax 2 to 1," United for a Fair Economy, August 31, 2005; www.faireconomy.org/press/2005/EstateTaxpr.html.

5. Estate Tax News, United for a Fair Economy, www.faireconomy.org/estatetax.

6. Estate Tax Polling, Coalition for America's Priorities, February 26, 2006; www.coalition4americaspriorities.com/pdfs/polling-20060226.pdf.

7. "Iowa/New Hampshire Democrats Talk Inheritance Taxes," Luntz, Maslansky Strategic Research, February 16, 2006; www.policyandtax ationgroup.com/pdf/LuntzSchoenNH-IAFeb06%20.pdf.

8. See my books *Healing ADD* (Underwood Books, 1998), *Focus Your Energy* (Pocket Books, 1994), *Beyond ADD: Hunting for Reasons in the Past and Present* (Underwood Books, 1996), and *ADD Success Stories: A Guide to Fulfillment for Families with Attention Deficit Disorder* (Underwood Books, 1995).

CHAPTER 11

LEARNING THE LEGEND

1. The first published reference to a "pro-choice" movement to protect the right to abortion appears to have been a story in the *Wall Street Journal* on March 20, 1975.

2. An excellent brief history of the legal cases and review of state laws, "Late-term Abortions: Legal Considerations," January 1997, is available on Guttmacher Institute Web site: http://www.guttmacher.org/pubs/ib13.html.

3. As of February 2007, per the Coalition for Positive Sexuality, http://www.positive.org/Resources/consent.html.

4. L. B. Finer and S. K. Henshaw, "Abortion Incidence and Services in the United States in 2000," *Perspectives on Sexual and Reproductive Health* (2003) 35(1): 6–15; http://www.guttmacher.org/pubs/fb_induced_abor tion.html.

CHAPTER 12

THE MOTIVATION CODE

1. Molly Moore and John Ward Anderson, "France Narrows Its Presidential Choices," *Washington Post,* April 23, 2007. Sarkozy's speech is also available in French on his Web site at www.sarkozy.fr.

2. Ibid. Royal's speech can be found in French on www.desirsdavenir.org (*désirs d'avenir* means "desires for the future").

3. This study compares the deaths of rats taking unlimited amounts of cocaine with those taking unlimited amounts of heroine but illustrates the point that rats will continue to take cocaine until they die—90 percent of rats in this study died. Michael A. Bozarth and Roy A. Wise, "Toxicity Associated with Long-term Intravenous Heroin and Cocaine Self-

administration in the Rat." *Journal of the American Medical Association* (1985) 254(1): 81–83; http://wings.buffalo.edu/aru/ARUreport06.htm.

4. Said to National Public Radio's Mara Liasson in a May 25, 2001, interview.

CHAPTER 13

CHUNKING THE CODE

1. Just a decade ago, the payback period was as high as twenty years. Most in the industry suggest that the payback period will be in the one- to three-year average range by 2010, which will make the argument in favor of solar a lot easier to make.

2. "The 100.000 Roofs Programme," case study #8, October 21, 2004; http://www.senternovem.nl/mmfiles/The%20100.000%20Roofs%20 Programme_tcm24-117023.pdf.

3. Preben Maegaard, "Sensational German Renewable Energy Law and Its Innovative Tariff Principles," June 20, 2000; http://www.folkecenter .dk/en/articles/EUROSUN2000-speech-PM.htm.

4. After passage of this law, solar companies generated revenues of $435 million in 2000. See Reiner Gaertner, "Germany Embraces the Sun," July 9, 2001; http://www.wired.com/news/technology/0,1282,450 56,00.html.

CHAPTER 14

THE IDENTITY CODE

1. See *Healing ADD* (Underwood Books, 1998), especially chapter 7. For a more detailed account of this kind of therapy, see Connirae Andreas, *Core Transformation: Reaching the Wellspring Within* (Real People Press, 1996).

2. The best way to find out who really uses a product is to read the marketing materials created for advertisers. Advertisers need to know precisely the demographics to whom they are selling. This is a marketing report created for the Irwindale Speedway to convince advertisers to buy into the NASCAR race market: http://www.irwindalespeedway .com/ISdemo05.pdf.

3. Ibid.

4. For a longer—and well-footnoted—discussion of the way the Bush administration uses fear to gain followers, see Jay Dixit, "The Ideological Animal," *Psychology Today*, January/February 2007; www.psychology today.com/articles/index.php?term=pto-20061222-000001&page=1.

5. From *The Bush Dyslexicon* (W. W. Norton, 2002, pp. 52–53).

6. "Face-to-face, Nixon-Kennedy," Vice President Richard M. Nixon and Senator John F. Kennedy, fourth joint television-radio broadcast, October 21, 1960; http://www.jfklibrary.org/Historical+Resources/Archives/ Reference+Desk/Speeches/JFK/JFK+Pre-Pres/fourth+televised +debate.htm.

CONCLUSION

RECLAIMING THE LIBERAL STORY

1. CNN/Opinion Research Corporation Poll, May 4–6, 2007; http://www .pollingreport.com/abortion.htm.

2. Of 994 adults polled nationwide, 48 percent think taxes are too high, 44 percent think they are about right, 2 percent think they are too low, and 5 percent are unsure. CBS News Poll, April 9–12, 2007; http://www .pollingreport.com/budget.htm.

3. ABC News/Washington Post/Stanford University Poll; April 5–10, 2007; http://www.pollingreport.com/enviro.htm.

4. CNN/Opinion Research Corporation Poll, May 4–6, 2007; http://www .pollingreport.com/iraq.htm.

5. Sarah Schweitzer, "Card Says President Sees America as a Child Needing a Parent," *Boston Globe*, September 2, 2004; http://www.boston.com/news/nation/articles/2004/09/02/ card_says_bush_sees_us_as_a_child_needing_a_parent.

INDEX

Acknowledgments

When I was six years old, a boy in my class accused me of stealing his pencil. Because all of the #2 pencils in the class looked the same, I was unable to rebut his loud and outraged suggestion that I had lost my pencil and taken his. The superiority of his communication convinced our teacher that I had, indeed, stolen his pencil, and she had me walk down a gauntlet of all the students in the class to approach him, at the end of the line, and hand him my pencil and apologize.

Telling my parents about it that evening, I burst into tears. Why would he say that I had stolen his pencil when he knew that I hadn't and he'd simply lost his own? And why would the teacher believe him instead of me? And what should I do about it?

My mother's wise advice (consistent with her degree from Michigan State University [MSU] in English literature) was to quote Shakespeare: "Whether 'tis nobler in the mind to suffer the slings and arrows of outrageous fortune, or to take arms against a sea of troubles..." She said that I'd done all I could in protesting my honesty and that over time my teacher and my peers would come to know that I was an honest person. This wasn't a fight worth extending, but, she said, I should retract my under-duress apology.

My father's take was along an altogether different line, that this was a good lesson learned. "Now you know that you can't trust him," my dad said of the other boy. He added, "People who are dishonest assume everybody else is. People who steal things assume that everybody else does. Notice in your life the people who assume things like that about others and know that they are the ones you should avoid. A person always worried about being robbed is probably a thief." The flipside of it, he said, was that "People who are truly trustworthy are people whose first impulse is to trust others." (My father was also one of the most trusting men I've ever known.)

My parents taught me the importance of communication, that just saying something without considering *how* it was said wasn't enough and that different people have very different views, stories, and experiences of the world. For that I'm indebted and grateful. Over the years since then, I've had a number of mentors in communication. My first partner in a "real" business, Terry O'Connor, who owned an advertising agency in Lansing, Michigan, and later taught the topic at MSU, introduced me to the world of systematically and intentionally framing communications. I learned so much from him and from professionals in the industry like Joe Sugarman and David Ogilvy that by the mid-1970s I was teaching advertising and marketing to employees of ad agencies across the country while also working part-time in the communication-based business of radio.

In 1978 I left the world of business to join my wife, Louise, in creating a community for abused children in New Hampshire and to do international relief work for a charity based in Germany, founded and run by my second mentor, Gottfried Müller. I wrote a book about him titled *The Prophet's Way;* he was one of the most masterful communicators I've met.

The psychology aspect of that work led me to study psychotherapy and Neuro-Linguistic Programming, a field from which much of the content (and many of the terms) in this book is derived. I commend to you the many books written by Richard Bandler, who was one of my best teachers, who trained and licensed me as an NLP trainer, and who wrote the foreword to my 1995 book on the use of NLP for attention deficit disorder, *Healing ADD.* Other personal teachers in that field were Hillel Zeitlin; Charles Ehrenpreis; Connirae, Tamara, and Steve Andreas; Leif Roland; and Paul McKenna.

Special thanks for the creation of this book goes to Jo Ellen Green Kaiser, who took many of my on-air and phone discussions and translated them into some of the chapters of this book, and to Susan Nethercott, who transcribed all of my original "Cracking the Code" radio program segments into writing for use by Jo Ellen and me. Jo Ellen also did a great job of tracking down and analyzing a number of campaign ads that were used as examples in this book. Thanks also to Johanna Vondeling at Berrett-Koehler Publishers, who believed in the need for this book and helped bring it to you. Special thanks also to the production team of Richard Wilson, Dianne Platner, Gary Palmatier, and Elizabeth von Radics for their dedication to their craft and their tireless commitment to quality on behalf of this book.

And, as with every book I've ever written, I owe huge thanks to my best editor and best friend, my wife, Louise Hartmann.

About the Author

Thom Hartmann is a three-time Project Censored–award winning, *New York Times* best-selling author of 20 books in print in 14 languages and the host of an Air America radio talk show. Formerly on the Vermont roster of psychotherapists, executive director of a residential treatment facility for severely emotionally disturbed and abused children, and a guest faculty member of Goddard College, he was also CEO of an Atlanta-based advertising agency and an advertising and marketing consultant to corporations and governments on five continents. Trained by Leif Roland, Paul McKenna, and Richard Bandler, he is licensed and certified as a Neuro-Linguistic Programming practitioner and an NLP trainer by the Society of Neuro-Linguistic Programming, and Bandler has written the foreword to one of his books. The father of three grown children, he lives in Portland, Oregon, with his wife, Louise, and their attack cat, Higgins.

AVAILABLE NOW!

SCREWED: *THE UNDECLARED WAR AGAINST THE MIDDLE CLASS... AND WHAT WE CAN DO ABOUT IT*

Nationally syndicated radio host and bestselling author Thom Hartmann exposes the covert war conservatives, and corporations are waging against America's middle class, a war that's reducing the rest of us to a politically impotent working poor. This book asks: How did this happen? Who's benefiting? And how can we stop it?

Available in paperback, and as a PDF download at www.bkconnection.com/screwed

THE BEST OF THOM HARTMANN PROGRAM DIGITAL AUDIO

Features excerpts from some of Thom's classic Air America shows, including conversations with bestselling authors from across the political spectrum.

Vol 1: *We the People*: Thom focuses on the state of American democracy-its historic roots and its present imperiled health.

Vol 2: *Our Living History*: Thom brings his deep grounding in American history to bear on current events.

Each volume of The Best of the Thom Hartmann Program is ninety minutes of thoughtful hard-hitting audio commentary and conversations.

Visit www.bkconnection.com/hartmannaudio to hear samples and purchase.

CRACKING THE CODE DIGITAL AUDIO

This unabridged audio includes a new foreword written and read by Jim Hightower

Visit www.bkconnection.com/crackingaudio for details.

Be Connected

Visit Our Web Site

Go to www.bkconnection.com to read exclusive previews and excerpts of new books, find detailed information on all Berrett-Koehler titles and authors, browse subject-area libraries of books, and get special discounts.

Subscribe to Our Free E-Newsletter

Be the first to hear about new publications, special discount offers, exclusive articles, news about bestsellers, and more! Get on the list for our free e-newsletter by going to www.bkconnection.com.

Get Quantity Discounts

Berrett-Koehler books are available at quantity discounts for orders of ten or more copies. Please call us toll-free at (800) 929-2929 or e-mail us at bkp.orders@aidcvt.com.

Host a Reading Group

For tips on how to form and carry on a book reading group in your workplace or community, see our Web site at www.bkconnection.com.

Join the BK Community

Thousands of readers of our books have become part of the "BK Community" by participating in events featuring our authors, reviewing draft manuscripts of forthcoming books, spreading the word about their favorite books, and supporting our publishing program in other ways. If you would like to join the BK Community, please contact us at bkcommunity@bkpub.com.